Cycles
of
Profit

Cycles
of
Profit

Jake Bernstein

HarperBusiness
A Division of HarperCollins*Publishers*

Library of Congress Cataloging-in-Publication Data

Bernstein, Jacob, 1946-
    Cycles of Profit / Jake Bernstein.
      p.   cm.
    ISBN 0-88730-471-0 : $29.95
    1. Stock-exchange.   2. Stocks—Charts, diagrams, etc.   3. Business
cycles. I. Title.
HG4551.B45 1991   91-8582
332.63′222—dc20   CIP

Printed in the United States of America

91 92 93 94 CC/HC 9 8 7 6 5 4 3 2 1

Contents

vi   Contents

The Yin-Yang view of the world is serenely cyclic. Fortune and misfortune, life and death . . . come and go everlastingly without beginning or end. . . . The forces are so interdependent that no one can exist without all of the others, just as there can be no yang without yin.

—Alan Watts

Introduction
The Importance of Trends

In August 1967 I was a college student at the University of Illinois in Champaign, Illinois, completing my undergraduate work in clinical psychology. I had little knowledge of stocks, economics, investing, and money. I had come to the United States from Canada with my family only eight years before, and we were not blessed with affluence. My parents had arrived in Canada penniless in 1949 following incarceration in Hitler's death camps of Dachau and Auschwitz, where both had lost their families. They would never return to their homeland, and they would never have the opportunity to complete a higher education. Instead, they barely managed to eke out a subsistence living in the slums of Montreal.

Following years of efforts to emigrate to the United States, my father serendipitously found employment as a tailor in the affluent North Shore Chicago suburb of Winnetka, Illinois, and my family moved from an area of abject poverty to one of the wealthiest areas in the world. When I studied sociology many years later, I found the term "culture shock" easily understandable. When my family moved to Winnetka, I was enrolled in the eighth grade. Although I had barely managed to stay in school in Canada, I found school in the United States extremely simple. What I seemingly had learned by osmosis in Canada, sitting in a classroom and never doing my homework, was more than enough to make me an above-average student in the United States. The paradox is still difficult for me to understand. But it is no wonder, that even a basic understanding of stocks and financial matters was not passed on to me by my parents as was the case for so many of my peers.

One of my first classroom projects in the eighth grade involved the

ix

stock market. Every student was given a fictitious $5,000 account. The task was to "invest" the money in stocks, to monitor the stocks weekly, and to report to the teacher on all "transactions." I was distressed but not too surprised to find that most of my fellow students were acquainted with the basic concepts of the stock market. Many of them already had their favorite stocks and were able to speak about the market, its trends, and such things as stock splits and blue chips, none of which I understood. I felt somewhat relieved when one of the students spoke about "utilities," a term familiar to me from many hours of playing the Parker Brothers "Monopoly" game.

For my first "investment," I bought some shares in IBM and Polaroid, thinking that I had better go with well-known names. I made my choices based on the yearly highs and lows for these stocks. I reasoned that I'd be doing right to buy a stock that had a name I recognized if it was well below its high for the year. Surely, a stock that was of good quality was likely to return to its previously high levels, perhaps surpass them. By buying near the low for the year I'd be getting a bargain. But alas, my stocks continued to decline. I realized then that "bodies in motion tend to stay in motion;" that perhaps I'd have been better off buying stocks that were making new highs for the year rather than in buying stocks that were at their lows for the year. I was intrigued by the idea but felt intimidated by my lack of knowledge and overwhelmed by the many other adjustments and changes occurring in my life. It was not until my college days that I had a more formal introduction to the stock market, and it was then that my serious studies began.

Why should my life story and early experiences with the stock market be of interest to you? For several reasons. First, I come to the markets from a background that is not traditionally American middle class or upper middle class. My understanding of life was shaped by hardship and poverty. I may, therefore, see things differently from what is traditional. In this day and age of sameness it may be good to hear the sound of a "different drummer."

Second, who I am has influenced the development of my market theories. My first experience with stocks, for example, taught me the importance of *trend* and the value of staying with the trend. Moreover, it stimulated me to seek methods and systems for determining when the existing trend has *changed*.

Finally, my background provides insight into why I consider market fundamentals to be relatively meaningless if we have the tools to properly determine trend. I was raised in an environment filled with "bad" fundamentals. In spite of these negative fundamentals I was able to change the trend of my life and to come from poverty to wealth by recognizing potential opportunities.

In order to remain successful, today's investor must be able to spot potential changes in trend either shortly before they occur or shortly after they occur. Once a trend has started in earnest, market psychology changes, and it is difficult for an investor to buy today what could have been bought earlier at less than half of today's price. Although this can and often should be done, it still takes discipline and an understanding of trend to enter the market during a strong trend. More typically, smaller investors tend to buy stocks as an uptrend ends or to sell of stocks near the end of a declining market. In both instances emotion rules supreme, and decisions are not made on the basis of technical or fundamental factors.

Following my first exposure to stocks, I had no further experiences with them until my third year of college. Good fortune sent me a dormitory roommate, John, who was an avid student of the stock market. His father, an attorney, had educated his son in the workings of the stock market, in the value of precious metals, and in a variety of techniques for finding stocks that were about to make large moves.

John was still under age and not able to open an account in his name. It was only after his constant badgering that I opened a small stock account with his money at the local office of what was then called Hayden-Stone Securities. Remembering my earlier experience with stocks I was nervous about opening the account. Yet I was impressed with John's dedication, fervor, and keen understanding of the markets. He didn't just read the *Wall Street Journal*—he studied it! He read every book, chart publication, article, or story on investing that he could get his hands on. He pored over prices, numbers, and statistics. Given his obvious commitment to the markets, I felt a little more assured that opening a stock account was the right thing to do.

We bought about 200 shares of a small Canadian gold mining stock, Wright-Hargraves, listed on the American Stock Exchange as WRT. It was selling at 3 and a few sixteenths. I must admit that it was exciting.

We'd go down to the broker's office and watch WRT go up or down a few sixteenths. We'd call for quotes. We looked at charts. I learned about the gold stocks, about the Canadian golds, about the South African golds, about what made gold go up and down. We saw it move up with the other gold stocks, and we watched it move down when the stock market began to rally. We even traded it a few times.

I learned to use price charts; how to read them, what they meant, and how to spot stocks that were likely to make big moves. I also finally understood the concept and mechanics of selling short. There couldn't have been a better way to learn than by actually owning some stock, and there couldn't have been a better way for John to get me "hooked" on the market than to actually open the account and trade. Although John and I parted company many years ago, I will forever be grateful to him for the many things he taught me about the markets.

My education was still incomplete. No matter how much I learned, no matter how much I understood about point-and-figure charts, trend lines, chart formations, and odd-lot short sales, I failed to comprehend one thing that John repeatedly pointed out to me. For several years I had heard him say, almost as an afterthought, "it depends on the direction of the market." Virtually every time we analyzed a stock, concluding its probable direction, John would end the conversation by saying, "It looks good, but it won't go up unless the market does. . . . It all depends on the direction of the market." Yet no matter how many times he said it, I didn't realize the importance of his words. On the few occasions I stopped to think about the importance of the overall market trend, I concluded that a good stock would go its own way regardless of trend. I failed to realize that a bullish stock might fail to rise or that it might rise only minimally in a bear market or that a bearish stock might not decline in a bull market, regardless of how bad the underlying fundamentals might be.

Slowly, however, I began to understand the real importance of overall market trends. Clearly, the investor, trader, or speculator was faced with a paradoxical task, a task that seemed simple on the surface but that was difficult to implement for a variety of reasons.

During the years that followed, I became interested in the futures markets and began to trade them quite actively. I found that many futures moved faster, required less margin, had a limited life span, and had their own market terminology, the key elements of stock and futures trading were much the same. My education in stocks proved to be an asset, but the most valuable lessons I had learned were about the importance of trend and the limits of fundamental information.

I remained active in the futures markets, and in 1972 I launched a futures trading newsletter that has been published every week since. In addition, I authored more than 12 texts about the markets including the following:

The Investor's Quotient. New York: John Wiley & Sons, 1980.

The Handbook of Commodity Cycles: A Window on Time. New York: John Wiley & Sons, 1982.

How to Profit in Precious Metals. New York: John Wiley & Sons, 1985.

Seasonal Concepts in Futures Trading. New York: John Wiley & Sons, 1986.

Beyond the Investor's Quotient. New York: John Wiley & Sons, 1986.

Facts on Futures. Chicago: Probus Publishing, 1987.

Short-Term Traders Manual. Chicago: Probus Publishing, 1987.

Cyclical Analysis in Futures Trading. New York: John Wiley & Sons, 1988.

The Analysis and Forecasting of Long-Term Trends. Chicago: Probus Publishing, 1989.

The New Prosperity. New York: New York Institute of Finance, 1989.

How The Futures Market Works. New York: New York Institute of Finance, 1989.

Jake Bernstein's Seasonal Futures Spreads. New York: John Wiley & Sons, 1990.

Since then, trial and error, as well as many years' worth of trading, research, and analysis, have taught me the following important lessons:

1. The major consideration in all markets, whether stocks, futures, or real estate, is the direction of the major trend.

2. My first task is therefore to determine the major trend of a given market or group of markets.

3. Individual markets within a broader industry or specialty group (for example, the gold stocks, the automobile stocks, precious metals futures, the Dow Industrials) tend to move in the direction of the group as a whole. Although not all issues within the group will move with it, a majority will.

4. When a given stock or issue within a broader group fails to move in the direction of the overall group, there is usually a good reason for its hesitation. Such information can be used to the advantage of the investor or trader.

5. The economy, the stock market, the futures markets, the real estate market, in fact, virtually all free markets move in predictable waves, patterns, and rhythms. These can be ascertained, projected, and employed to either forecast changes in trend or recognize when a trend change is likely to be significant or secular, as opposed to short-lived or ephemeral.

6. The underlying causes or fundamentals of a given market may or may not have an immediate effect on the price of the given market.

7. Markets tend to anticipate fundamentals and news, and by the time news and fundamentals are generally known, it is often too late to take advantage of them.

8. Items one through five, when considered as a total investment or trading approach, can prove highly profitable for investor and speculator alike.

The balance of this book focuses on my cyclical theories and studies of the stock market. My discussion is directed at the pragmatic application of cyclical concepts and indicators. I do not spend much time on theories. Instead, I explain specific stock market cycles, providing concise illustrations and examples.

Acknowledgments

A special note of thanks to Commodity Quote Graphics and Aspen Research for permission to use their charts; and to the Foundation for the Study of Cycles for their excellent research, as well as their permission to quote extensively from their publications. Thanks also to all the others who have contributed to my efforts.

Cycles
of
Profit

Chapter 1

An Introduction to Repetitive Market Patterns

After a time of decay comes the turning point. The powerful light that has been banished returns. There is movement, but it is not brought about by force . . . the movement is natural, arising spontaneously. For this reason the transformation of the old becomes easy. The old is discarded and the new is introduced. Both measures accord with the time; therefore no harm results.

—From the *I Ching*

While the transformation is taking place, the declining culture refuses to change, clinging ever more rigidly to its outdated ideas; nor will the dominant social institutions hand over their leading roles to the new cultural forces. But they will inevitably go on to decline and disintegrate while the rising culture will continue to rise, and eventually will assume its leading role. As the turning approaches, the realization that evolutionary changes of this magnitude cannot be prevented by short-term political activities provides our strongest hope for the future.

—Fritjof Capra, *The Turning Point*

While the above quotes from the opening and conclusion of Fritjof Capra's *The Turning Point*[1] refer to social and cultural changes, cyclical patterns and changes are readily observable in virtually every aspect of life, nature, and science. Patterns, cycles, and seasonal variations have been with us since prehistoric times. Early civilizations developed numerous systems for tracking time based on astronomical cycles. In *The Analysis and Forecasting of Long-Term Trends,*[2] I commented on the history of cycles and civilization:

---

1. Capra, F., *The Turning Point* (New York: Bantam Books, 1982).
2. Bernstein, J., *The Analysis and Forecasting of Long-Term Trends* (Chicago: Probus Books, 1989), 105–06.

Repetition, patterns in time, and rhythm are key elements in the structure of our universe. The 24-hour day, the endless orbits of the planets around the sun, and the approximate 22,000 year "wobble" of the earth round its axis are gross examples of repetitive events in our lives. But just as many of the things we do frequently become "automatic" or somewhat reflexive, the cycles which surround us are frequently not given too much thought or consideration. Through the aeons the cyclic processes within and without ourselves have become so internalized that we rarely stop to consider either their cause, origin, or regulatory mechanisms. Yet they are omnipresent, regulating the functioning of our biological machinery, our environment, and our universe. Some 20,000 to 30,000 years ago Ice Age people in the Upper Paleolithic period marked the passage of time by scratching notches on what Archaeologists have called the Blanchard Bone. What was originally thought to be decorative marks or hunting tallies was according to Alexander Marshack a complex record of lunar phases inscribed by Aurignacian cave dwellers. This most incredible historical record housed at the Musée des Antiquités Nationales in Paris bears witness to the fact cycles and repetitive patterns have for many years been tracked and employed by humankind. But for what purpose?

The continued study of megaliths such as the well-known Stonehenge, and the lesser-known Woodhenge, Gors Fawr and Long Meg and Her Daughters provide evidence that time-based repetitive phenomena have long occupied the interest and energy of our ancestors. But why? The answer is a simple one indeed, one which we in our "progress" have either long forgotten or to which we now assign little importance. The answer has been eclipsed by the pace of modern technology, scientific progress, and the "growth" of "civilization." The answer is simply that the passage of time reflects the underlying processes of all life forms, all achievement, and all physical systems. In another dimension, in another place, time may not exist. In this plane, however, we are captives of matter, energy, space, and time as formulated mathematically by Albert Einstein in his special theory of relativity. Time is the most obvious dimension of our existence. Events are marked by time. Timing, the passage of time, aging, speed as measured in miles per hour or milliseconds, reaction time, computer time, atomic clocks, the 30-minute sit-com with six minutes of commercials, 91-day T-bills, 10-year T-Notes, Soviet Five-Year Plans, prison terms, leases—we are surrounded by time. We are products of time and prisoners of time. We take time for granted. We realize we have only limited time. Some of us seek to buy time, to reverse the aging process. But options eventually reach their expiration date. They lose their premium, decay, and expire. Time measures the patterns of growth in all organisms, microscopic and macroscopic. In our enlightenment we readily embrace the patterns and cycles of astronomy, chemistry, physics, and biology. Yet we are reticent to accept the fact that economies, prices, and business are also systems which follow the time-based growth cycles exhibited by biological systems.

In their now classic work, *Cycles: The Science of Prediction,* Dewey and Dakin attempted to convince the business world that cycles play a key role in the rise and fall of prices, sales, inventories, and economic trends.

In spite of the brilliant arguments they advanced, in spite of the fact that they clearly demonstrated the pragmatic value of cycles, and in spite of the fact that even *Time* magazine recognized Ned Dewey as an "accurate enough prophet . . ." the 1980s still find a great majority of business people, politicians, and economists either ignorant of or unwilling to recognize the value of cyclic events in the worlds of finance, investment, business, and economics. The *New York Times* reviewed the work of Dewey and Dakin, stating "Businessmen and students of economic dynamics alike will do well not to dismiss them lightly." Either there weren't too many readers, the cyclic ideas were too far ahead of their time, or more likely the ideas were too threatening to accept. The fact remains that in today's "civilized" world cycles are still not accepted by most investors, analysts, economists, social scientists, politicians, or traders as viable, practical, or potentially profitable.

I have studied cycles and cyclical analysis since the early 1970s, and have arrived at a number of conclusions that tend to refute traditionally accepted fundamentals of stock market analysis. Although fundamentalists and technicians have long been at odds, and I don't expect their debate to come to a quick resolution, both approaches to market analysis have their advantages and disadvantages.

Edward R. Dewey, the father of cyclical analysis, published considerable material on cyclical tendencies in the stock market. In order to further the study and dissemination of cyclical research he founded the Foundation for the Study of Cycles, which has researched cycles in everything from stocks and sunspots to tree rings in Java and the abundance of lynx. Most of the Foundation's research and publications have been devoted to the stock market. The many cycles in stock prices and other socioeconomic data appear in Dewey's *Selected Writings* (figures 1.1 and 1.2).

FIGURE 1.1   *Fifty- to Sixty-Year and Twenty-five- to Thirty-year Cycles**

50-year cycle	• in war	54.5-year cycle
• in commodity prices	• in wheat prices	• in stock prices
and wars	53.500-year cycle	(railroad)
• in manufacturing	• in agricultural	54.6-year cycle
production	workers' wages	• in stock prices
• in wholesale prices	• in bank deposits	(railroad)
50- to 60-year cycle	• in coal consumption	57-year cycle
• in agricultural	• in coal production	• in international
workers' wages	• in consols (British)	battles
• in bank deposits	value	61.4-year cycle
• in Bank of France	• in copper prices	• in international
portfolio	• in cotton acreage	battles
• in coal consumption	• in devaluation in	24-year cycle
• in coal production	England	• in wheat prices
• in coal miners'	• in economic affairs	25-year cycle
wages	• in interest rates	• in building
• in cotton acreage	• in lead production	26.1-year cycle
• in copper prices	• in oat acreage	• in stock prices
• in exports	• in pig iron	(railroad)
• in imports	production	26.2745-year cycle
• in interest rates	• in prices	• in stock prices
• in lead production	• in rent in France	27.966-year cycle
• in oat acreage	• in river run off	• in post office
• in pig iron	• in ship building	revenues
production	• in textile workers	30-year cycle
• in prices	• in trade (foreign)	• in building
• in ship building	• deposits	• in stock prices
• in trade (foreign)	• in wheat prices	(railroad)

*Dewey, E. R., *Selected Writings* (Pittsburgh: Foundation for the Study of Cycles, 1970), 76.

In his classic work *Cycles: The Science of Prediction*[3] Dewey and his colleague Edwin F. Dakin made the following observations about what they termed "a new approach to economics and the problem of economic forecast":

The study here falls into two parts. First, it shows that rhythm and periodicity exist in the natural world, and that our economic world,

---

3. Dewey, E. R., and Dakin, E. F., *Cycles: The Science of Prediction* (Pittsburgh: Foundation for the Study of Cycles, Irvine, CA 1957), xi.

FIGURE 1.2 *Approximate Eighteen- to Nineteen-Year Cycles*

17.92-year cycle
- in sunspot numbers, alternate cycles reversed

17.93- or 17.94-year cycle
- in sunspot numbers, alternate cycles reversed

18-year cycle
- in bank credit
- in bricks
- in building activity
- in building construction
- in building materials
- in building permits
- in coal consumption and production
- in fir timber imported
- in furniture
- in loans and discounts
- in lumber production
- in panics
- in pig iron consumption and production
- in purchasing power
- in railroad expenditures
- in railroad freight revenue
- in railroad receivership
- in real estate activity
- in sheet glass retained
- in stock prices

18–20-year cycle
- in buildings demolished

18.2-year cycle
- in building activity and construction
- in immigration
- in industrial companies
- in loans and discounts
- in marriages
- in natural science phenomena
- in panics
- in pig iron
- in a public utility company sales
- in real estate activity
- in sales of an industrial company
- in stock prices
- in stock prices (industrial)

18.2–18.3-year cycle
- in construction
- in economic phenomena
- in floods, Nile River
- in immigration
- in an industrial company
- in loans and discounts
- in marriages
- in panics
- in pig iron
- in public utility company

- in real estate activity
- in stocks (industrial)

18.33-(18⅓)-year cycle
- in building activity and construction
- in building permits
- in buildings (residential)
- in discounts and loans
- in freight traffic (Canadian Pacific Railway)
- in furniture produced
- in an industrial company
- in lumber production
- in marriage rates
- in panics
- in pig iron
- in pig iron production
- in production
- in real estate activity
- in residential permits
- in sales of an industrial company
- in sales of a public utility company
- in stock prices
- in wheat acreage

18.3562-year cycle
- in stock prices

18.539-year cycle
- in post office revenues

19-year cycle
- in stock prices

analyzed with similar statistical tools, also displays curvilinear forms and distinct rhythms. Second, it deals with some of the ideas which underlie these facts, suggests implications which seem safely implicit in them, and indicates some meanings which such facts hold for all of us.

Following an extensive discussion of cycles in natural phenomena, covering subjects as diverse as sunspots and the abundance of salmon, the authors examine numerous economic cycles, including several cycles in the stock market, the foremost of which is the approximate nine-year cycle. Dewey and Dakin offer two graphs as supportive evidence for what they term the "nine-year rhythm in common stock prices" (see figures 1.3 and 1.4).

Additional evidence offered in support of the nine-year cycle is the approximate fifty-four-year cycle, which consists of six repetitions of the nine-year cycle in stocks, and the nine-year cycle in wholesale prices as shown in figure 1.5, also from the Dewey and Dakin work.

FIGURE 1.3   *Cycles in U.S. Common Stock Prices*

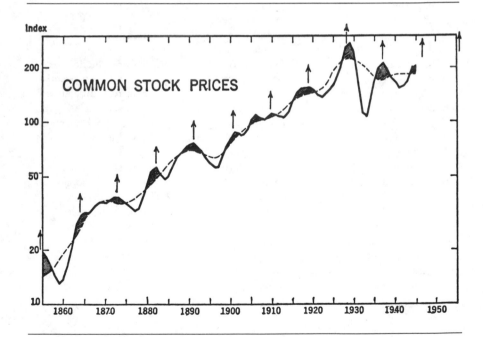

Source: Dewey and Dakin (1957),

FIGURE 1.4 *Nine-Year Cycles in Stock Prices: Deviations from Trend*

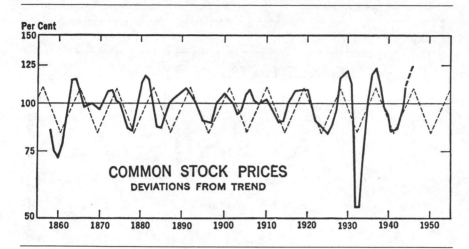

Source: Dewey and Dakin (1957),

Dewey and Dakin were not, however, the first to demonstrate the existence of cyclical patterns or rhythms in economic events or data series. W. L. Crum, Chapin Hoskins, Joseph Kitchin, and Joseph Schumpeter all provided substantial evidence that cyclical tendencies could be observed in interest rates, economic trends, and a variety of business-related phenomena. In fact, Kitchin, in a significant study, provides statistical evidence of an approximate 3.5-year cycle in wholesale prices and interest rates in Great Britain and the United States.[4] His 1923 article offers a detailed data list as well as graphic evidence (see figures 1.6 and 1.7).

By now, you probably are beginning to see the emergence of an interesting pattern. The fifty-four-year cycle, which is the "grandaddy" of economic cycles, consists of about six repetitions of an approximate nine-year period. The nine-year cycles consist of about two to three approximate 3.5-year rhythms. We can, in fact, reduce the 3.5-year, or so-called business cycle to approximately three cycles of about eleven months in length. Students of futures markets have learned that most

---

4. Kitchin, J., "Cycles and Trends in Economic Factors" *Review of Economic Statistics* 5 (1) (1923): 10–16.

FIGURE 1.5   *The Fifty-Four (a) and Nine-Year (b) Cycles in Wholesale Prices According to Dewey*

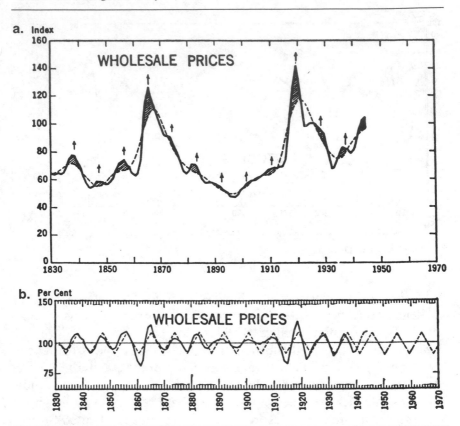

Source: Dewey and Dakin (1957),

markets exhibit an approximate eleven-month cycle as well. In other words, there are cycles within cycles, within cycles, within cycles. The nesting of these cycles is shown in figure 1.8.

But Dewey, Dakin, and Kitchin are not alone in their work. Other cyclical stock market analysts include N. D. Kondratieff, Simon Kuznets, W. W. Rostow, J. Tinbergen, J. J. Van Duijn, and W. C. Mitchell—none of whom has succeeded in convincing a skeptical investment world of the value of cyclical patterns and analysis. The reasons for this skepticism are examined in chapter 18.

FIGURE 1.6 *Kitchin Cycle in Graphic Form*

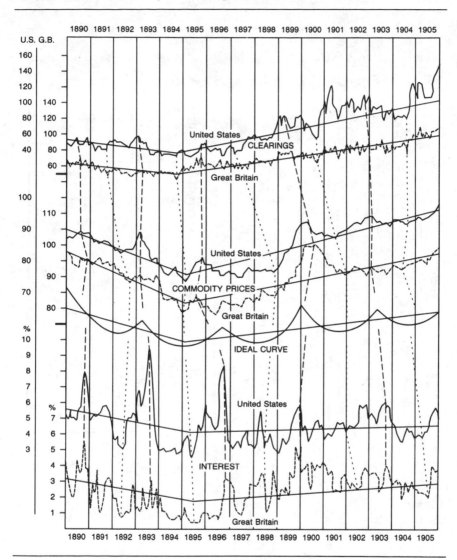

Source: Kitchin (1923),

Among the many contemporary proponents of cyclical analysis, the most notable is Jay W. Forrester of the Massachusetts Institute of Technology Systems Dynamics Group, who, armed with state-of-the-

FIGURE 1.7 Kitchin's 3.20- to 3.36-year cycle: Original Statistics

SCHEDULE OF MAXIMA AND MINIMA, 1890–1922

The ideal dates have their origin at the beginning of 1800, the maxima being placed 3.33 years apart and the minima midway between. Dates of minima are placed in italics. The dates of maxima and minima are years and fractions of years, representing monthly averages, except for Great Britain's prices and interest, which are end-monthly. Where virtual instead of actual monthly maxima or minima are selected, they are indicated by *.

The figures below each date are index numbers on the basis of 1900–13 = 100 for the following factors for the United States and Great Britain, respectively:
United States bank clearings—1900–13 monthly average, $11,750,000,000. Charted in units of $100,000,000.
Wholesale prices of commodities—Bureau of Labour 1900–22 as revised from 1913 (index 90 for 1900–13 on present basis of 1913 = 100), and 10 commodities 1890–99, as given in *Review of Economic Statistics*, vol. 3, p. 369, but condensed to agree approximately with Bureau of Labour annual figures.

Interest rate on 60- to 90-day commercial paper, New York—1900–13 average, 4.82 percent.
London bankers' clearing house returns—1900–13 monthly average, £1,037,000,000. Charted in units of £10,000,000.
Wholesale prices of commodities—Sauerbeck-Statist. 1900–13 average of 75.5 charted as 100.
Market rate of interest on three months' bills, London—1900–13 average, 3.26 percent.

Ideal Dates	United States			Great Britain		
	Clearings	Prices	Interest	Clearings	Prices	Interest
1890.00	1890.37	1890.62	1890.87	1890.54	1890.83	1890.83
	49	90	170	69	96	177
1891.67	*1891.62	*1892.37*	*1892.45*	*1891.62*	*1892.75*	*1892.49*
	35	*82*	*61*	*49*	*88*	*27*
1893.33	1893.04	1893.12	1893.54	1893.20	1893.16	1893.66
	51	89	202	56	91	96
1895.00	*1894.71*	*1895.20*	*1895.45*	*1894.71*	*1895.08*	*1895.57*
	30	*74*	*55*	*44*	*79*	*17*

Intervals in Years Between Maxima and Minima, Respectively

United States			Great Britain		
Clearings	Prices	Interest	Clearings	Prices	Interest
2.67	2.50	2.67	2.66	2.33	2.83
3.09	2.83	3.00	3.09	2.25	3.08
2.75	2.67	3.25	2.59	2.55	3.17

1896.67	1895.79 45	1895.79 82	1896.79 178	1895.79 71	*1895.71 84	*1896.83 100	2.41	3.76	3.00	2.74	3.75	2.92
1898.33	1897.12 31	*1898.96 77	*1898.45 67	*1897.45 56	*1898.83 84	*1898.49 31	3.41	4.41	3.17	3.75	4.87	3.08
1900.00	1899.20 74	1900.20 93	1899.96 122	*1899.54 80	1900.58 101	1899.91 173	3.59	2.49	3.67	3.26	3.17	4.00
1901.67	1900.71 49	1901.45 88	*1902.12 83	1900.71 64	1902.00 91	*1902.49 75	3.59	2.92	3.75	3.50	2.67	3.84
1903.33	*1902.79 96	1903.12 96	1903.71 124	1903.04 89	1903.25 93	1903.75 121	3.91	3.34	3.33	4.00	2.49	3.08
1905.00	*1904.62 68	1904.79 92	1905.45 78	*1904.71 75	1904.49 92	1905.57 56	4.25	4.67	4.25	4.00	4.16	4.16
1906.67	*1907.04 128	1907.79 108	1907.96 166	1907.04 116	1907.41 109	1907.91 188	3.50	3.83	4.00	3.91	4.67	3.92
1908.33	1908.12 75	1908.62 100	1909.45 67	1908.62 87	1909.16 95	1909.49 37	3.00	2.41	2.83	3.25	2.84	2.92
1910.00	1910.04 146	1910.20 110	1910.79 115	1910.29 132	1910.25 105	*1910.83 134	3.59	2.75	2.67	3.00	2.41	3.00
1911.67	*1911.71 107	1911.37 105	*1912.12 78	1911.62 109	*1911.57 104	*1912.49 73	2.75	3.51	2.75	2.50	3.00	3.00
1913.33	1912.79 146	1913.71 113	*1913.54 126	1912.79 145	1913.25 115	1913.83 152	2.91	4.08	3.75	3.00	3.92	2.59
1915.00	1914.62 84	*1915.45 110	1915.87 62	1914.62 65	*1915.49 141	1915.08 46	4.17	3.91	5.17	4.33	4.24	2.74
1916.67	*1916.96 233	1917.62 210	1918.71 124	1917.12 171	*1917.49 239	1916.57 172	4.50	3.67	3.25	4.67	3.84	4.41
1918.33	*1919.12 220	*1919.12 214	1919.12 108	*1919.20 182	*1919.33 244	1919.49 97	3.00	2.75	2.08	3.08	2.84	4.59
1920.00	1919.96 360	1920.37 274	1920.79 166	1920.20 353	1920.33 352	1921.16 208	2.00	2.92	3.50	2.42	2.83	3.08

FIGURE 1.7 *Continued*

Ideal Dates	United States			Great Britain			Intervals in Years Between Maxima and Minima, Respectively					
							United States			Great Britain		
	Clearings	Prices	Interest	Clearings	Prices	Interest	Clearings	Prices	Interest	Clearings	Prices	Interest
1921.67	1921.12	1922.04	1922.62	1921.71	*1922.16	1922.57						
	227	153	81	254	175	55						
Average interval between successive maxima 1890–1922							3.29	3.31	3.32	3.30	3.28	3.37
Average interval between successive minima 1890–1922							3.28	3.30	3.35	3.34	3.27	3.34
Average interval between successive maxima 1800–1913							3.20	3.30	3.24	3.19	3.20	3.29
Average interval between successive minima 1800–1913							3.35	3.17	3.28	3.33	3.14	3.33

Source: Kitchin (1923), 11.

FIGURE 1.8 *Cycle Lengths and Nesting of Cycles*

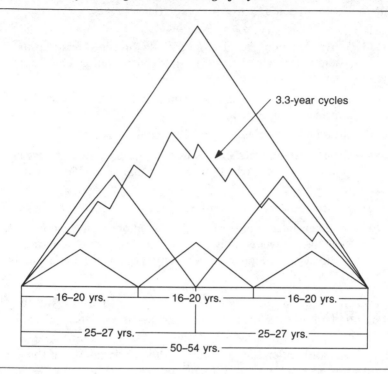

art computer technology and a vast statistical data base, has clearly demonstrated the validity of the long-wave, or fifty- to sixty-year, economic cycle.

The enigmatic J. M. Hurst caused a stir among market technicians and investors when he released his 1970 book *The Profit Magic of Stock Transaction Timing.* [5] His training as a mathematician and twenty-five years of experience in aerospace engineering and computers led him to formulate an intricate methodology that uses cyclical patterns for timing stock market entry and exit. He summarizes his general theoretical approach as follows (Hurst 1973: 48):

---

5. Hurst, J. M., *The Profit Magic of Stock Transaction Timing* (Englewood Cliffs, NJ: Prentice-Hall, 1970).

A large percentage of the price motion of all stocks consists of the
sum of a number of periodic-cyclic "waves."

The waves in each stock have many common characteristics, including duration, relative magnitude-duration relationships,
and a strong tendency to be time synchronized. This feature
can be expressed as a principle of commonality.

Deviations from commonality are minor and can be expressed as a
principle of variation.

Very little of stock price change is random in nature.

Smooth, underlying trends are caused by fundamental factors related to the growth of the economy and of specific industries
and companies.

Major historical events do not significantly influence the market.

Relative independence of stock price fluctuations from random and
historical events, plus the periodic and common nature of
the cyclic components permit timing analysis on a purely
"technical" basis.

Hurst's theories and methods attracted a wide following among simi-
larly minded investors, even as rumors about his disappearance cir-
culated throughout the trading community. The clarity, specificity,
trading rules, and concise suggestions of his work answered the dreams
of many investors who lacked an organized methodology for putting
their ideas to work. Figures 1.9 and 1.10 illustrate Hurst's contention
that stock market cycles exist and that they are independent of historical events. Hurst's own conclusions about cyclicality demonstrate the
appeal of his work (Hurst 1973: 157):

You don't need to understand the causes of price change in detail
in order to profit by the price-motion model—but it helps
when the unexpected occurs.

The traditional concepts of risk versus trading interval are out-dated
by the existence of the price-motion model.

The determining element of price change is the human decision-
making process.

Decision-making is complex and little understood. Emotions and
unrelated influences often play a large part. The unknowns
in the process probably mask the true cause of price motion
cyclicality.

FIGURE 1.9   *The Approximate Four-Year Cycle in Stocks According to Hurst*

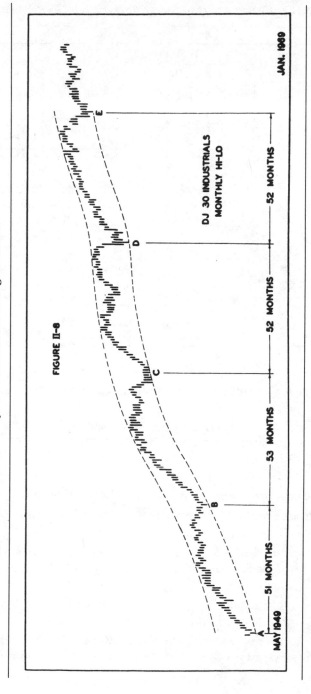

Source: Hurst (1973), 43.

FIGURE 1.10 *Hurst's Chart of Stock Market Cycles and World Events*

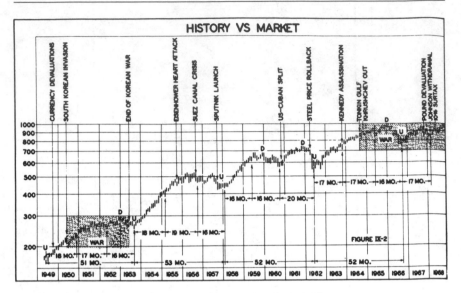

How History <u>Does Not</u> Influence The Market!

Source: Hurst (1953), 148.

Although the cause of cyclicality is unknown, the nature of the effect is certain.

The implications of cyclicality include possible external influence of the decision processes of masses of investors more or less simultaneously. If this is fact, you must guard yourself carefully against the same influences.

Cyclicality is probably not related to rational decision factors.

The lack of relationship between cyclicality and historical events is clear-cut.

More specific fundamental events cause wide differences in individual stock price action, and must always be taken into account.

There may be a link between gross national product and non-cyclic price action in the market.

True panics due to wars, currency devaluations, etc., represent buying opportunities if the cyclic picture is also ripe.

The extent of non-random cyclicality precludes any major contribution to price action by random events.

All price fluctuations about smooth long-term trends in the market (as represented by the DJIA) are due to manifestations of cyclicality.

Further examples of cycles in stocks and economic data are shown in figures 1.11 and 1.12.

Based on the examples and illustrations discussed to this point, cycles appear to have the following general characteristics:

1. *Repetition.* Cycles tend to move from a low point to a high point and back to a low point again in fairly regular time spans from low to low and from high to high.

2. *Regularity.* Cycles in economic data tend to move in fairly regular intervals from low to low, from low to high, and from high to low. Although not perfectly regular, cycles show a tendency toward regularity.

3. *Predictability.* Inasmuch as cycles are fairly regular, they are predictable within reasonable limits.

4. *Harmonics.* There are cycles within cycles within cycles. Cycles tend to occur in multiples of and in fractions of each other. If there is a four-year cycle, then there is probably an eight-year cycle; if there is a three-year cycle, then there are probably three to four nine- to eleven-month cycles in each three-year cycle.

In a previous book[6] which dealt with commodity prices I have demonstrated the existence of long-term, intermediate-term, and short-term cyclical tendencies in grain and livestock, metals, foreign currencies, and stock index futures. Cycles can be found in commodity prices (both cash and futures), as well as stocks and the stock market. As further examples of cyclical tendencies in commodity prices and financial markets, consider figures 1.13 through 1.16, which show long-term cycles in cash, sugar, beef steer, wheat, and soybean prices. When you return to these figures after reading several chapters of this book, you'll discover that the cyclical lengths for stocks, stock indices, commodity

---

6. Bernstein, J., *The Handbook of Commodity Cycles* (New York: Wiley, 1982), and *Cyclic Analysis in Futures Trading* (New York: Wiley, 1982).

FIGURE 1.11   *Cycles in Economic Indicators*

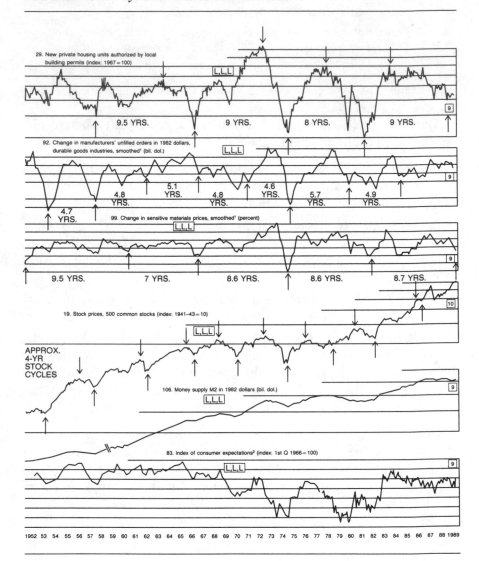

Source: U.S. Department of Commerce. BCD. (Oct. 1989), 13.

prices, and financial data are similar. If you understand cycles in stocks, then you also will understand cycles in commodities, financial data, and the economy. The markets are interrelated in one grand cyclical

FIGURE 1.12 *The Approximate Twenty-six Month Cycle in USAir Group*

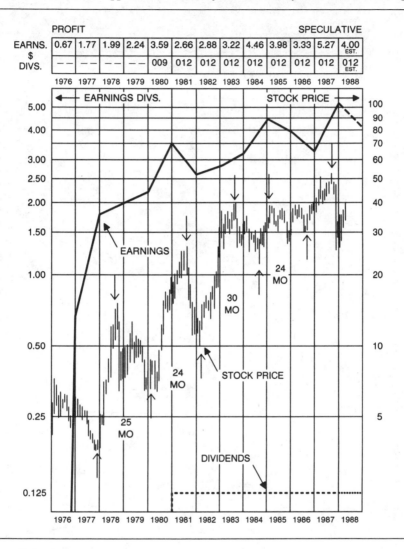

	PROFIT											SPECULATIVE
EARNS. $	0.67	1.77	1.99	2.24	3.59	2.66	2.88	3.22	4.46	3.98	3.33	5.27	4.00 EST.
DIVS.	— —	— —	— —	— —	009	012	012	012	012	012	012	012	012 EST.
	1976	1977	1978	1979	1980	1981	1982	1983	1984	1985	1986	1987	1988

Source: Babson's Report

scheme. But because cycles in stocks and other economic data vary from their ideal or average lengths, timing is another important consideration when using them for trading, investing, or speculating. Timing is discussed in considerable detail in chapter 8.

FIGURE 1.13　*The 7.63 Year Cycle in Cash Sugar Prices 1929–1991*

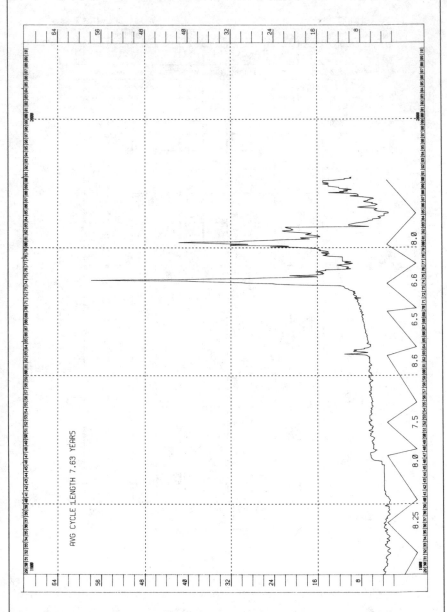

AVG CYCLE LENGTH 7.63 YEARS

Source:

FIGURE 1.14 *The 10.6 Year Cycle in Cattle Prices 1910–1991*

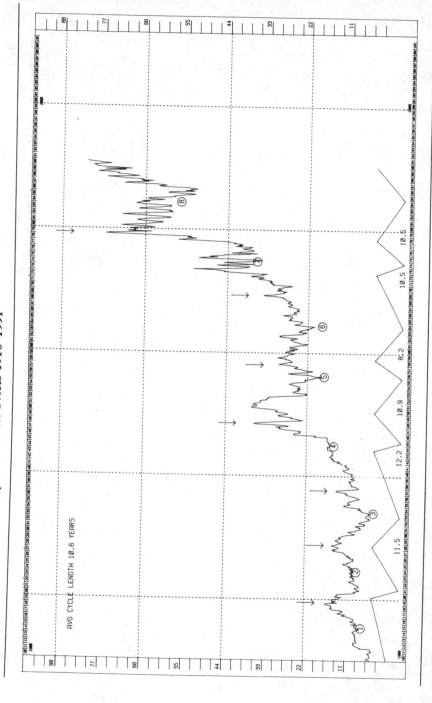

Numbers 1–8 mark cycle lows

FIGURE 1.15 *The 8.9 Year Cycle in Wheat 1910–1991*

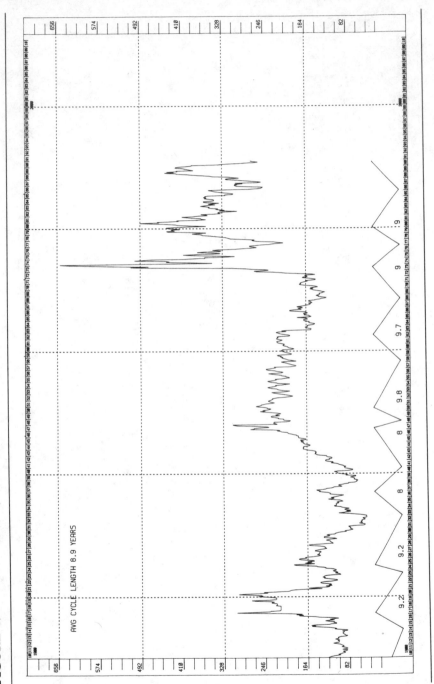

Source:

FIGURE 1.16 *Long Term Cycles in Cash Soybean Prices 1930–1991*

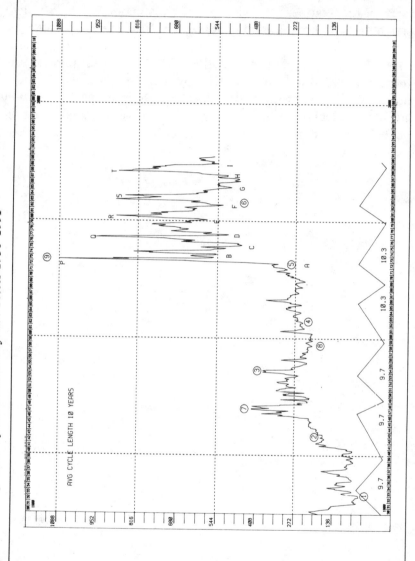

Numbers 1–9 show 10-year cycle highs and lows. Letters A–I show approximate 3-year cycle highs and lows

The preponderance of cycles in virtually all other data series strongly suggests that their effect can be detected in stock prices. I feel that the case for cycles in stocks is certainly a strong one, yet readers should not presume that the existence of cyclical tendencies in stock prices is a panacea for the treatment of unsuccessful investing or a "magic bullet" that guarantees high profits and no losses. Cyclical analysis and the use of cyclical tendencies are merely tools employed by the disciplined investor. Be aware of the fact that there are those who question the existence of cycles in stock prices, claiming that the movement of stocks is random. The value of these tools can be realized only as a function of the individual who uses the tools. Now let's turn to an examination of cycle characteristics.

Chapter 2

The Characteristics of Cycles

This chapter examines the characteristics of cycles in stocks and various economic phenomena and also provides important definitional groundwork for later chapters. As you will discover, cyclic analysis employs a precise and, in most cases, self-explanatory vocabulary.

What Is a Cycle?

Chapter 1 introduced specific cycles in various economic data. Because cycles constitute repetitive phenomena, their most pragmatic aspect is their relative predictability. In addition to this valuable characteristic, however, cycles have other qualities as well. Here is a listing of additional features of cycles:

1. *Period.* The time elapsed between cycle turns is referred to as the *period* or *time span.* Typically, the distance from low to low is measured in units of time.

2. *Reliability* of a cycle, or its usefulness in predicting future behavior, increases with its repetitions. Look for at least four repetitions of a cycle before assuming that a cyclic tendency exists, but attempt to find as many repetitions as possible.

3. *Synchronicity.* A cyclic relationship between two seemingly unrelated markets is called *synchronicity.*

4. *Harmonics* are the cycles which are fractional lengths of long cycles in the same data series.

5. *Interrelationships* are the similarities in cycle lengths that can be found in more than one market.

6. *Magnitude.* Cycle length measures time between cycle waves, and *magnitude* measures the height of cycle waves.

7. *Independence from fundamentals.* Cycles tend to lead economic events and are usually independent of fundamental events.

8. *Persistence.* Cycles endure over time and compensate for certain influences by shortening or lengthening a cycle repetition.

Other aspects of cycles—such as confluence, lead, and lag are not as operationally concise. Cyclical analysis is not a rigorously scientific set of procedures, but acquiring a general knowledge of cycles and market timing techniques is the best tool we have for developing an effective orientation to stock trend analysis.

Stocks, Cycles, and the News

Perhaps the most perplexing aspect of cycles is their tendency to turn when fundamental conditions appear to offer the least likelihood of a turn: bottoms tend to come when news is bad, and tops tend to come when news is good. It may be relatively painless to accept this fact intellectually, but it is a psychological paradox. Legendary stock and futures trader W. D. Gann expressed the situation as follows:[1]

> Every time stocks made bottom, the newspapers, government officials and economists said that it was the last bottom, but stocks went down, down, down, until people lost faith and hope in everything. They went lower than anybody dreamed they could go. That is what happens when everybody decides that stocks cannot go down or that stocks cannot go up—they always do the opposite. The public is always wrong, because they follow no well-defined rule and are not organized. People believed that the Government by buying cotton, wheat and loaning money could stop the depression, but when once a cycle is up and prices are due to decline, nothing can stop them until it has run its course. The same when the main trend turns up, neither government interference nor anything else can stop the advance until it runs its course.
> Every investor and trader should do his own studying and learn rules

---

1. Gann, W. D., *How to Make Money in Stocks.* (Greenville, S.C. Traders Press, 1949), 91.

and apply them and not rely on other people who know no more about the market than he does.

In order to successfully employ cyclical tendencies in the stock market you need to adhere to the following general rules:

1. Expect a bottom when a majority of investors, the public, the media, and professionals are negative and expect prices to continue lower.

2. Expect a top when a majority of investors, the public, the media, and professionals are optimistic and expect prices to continue higher.

3. When cyclical tops are expected and the news and fundamentals are positive, the odds of a significant top are greatest.

4. When cyclical bottoms are expected and the news and fundamentals are negative, the odds of a significant bottom are greatest.

5. To take advantage of such major turning points apply both methodological and psychological discipline by ignoring feelings of optimism or fear and adhering strictly to the timing and trend rules discussed in this book.

6. Do your market work regularly in order to take advantage of opportunities when they present themselves.

7. Keep your work relatively simple and basic to avoid the trap of being lost in complicated formulas, interpretations of fundamentals, and uncertainty prompted by subjective indicators and theories.

The Time Window Concept

Cyclical analysis in the financial markets and in the economy is a relatively young and inexact discipline. There is no universally accepted methodological approach to cyclical analysis. Instead, many different techniques are used to find and apply cycles, ranging from simple visual observation to complex mathematical extrapolation. Moreover, there is no one-to-one correlation between efficacy and complexity in these methods of cyclical analysis. The complex and computerized approaches may have scientific appeal, but they frequently are impractical and beyond the reach of the average investor both in their complexity and cost. All the techniques discussed in this book are simple to understand, equally simple to apply, and cost effective in terms of production. By the last point I mean that it won't cost you dearly to generate the charts and statistics needed to employ cyclical analysis in your investment program.

The building block of my approach is what I have termed the *time window*. Basically a window of opportunity, the time window is a span of time during which a change in market cycle trend is likely to occur based on the historical cyclical tendency in a given stock or group of stocks (such as the Dow Jones averages or the Standard & Poor's averages). A simple analogy can help further clarify the time window concept.

As an investor you know that market timing is important. You may correctly expect a market to move in a given direction, but if you prematurely enter the market or buy a given stock, you may have to sit through a move against you—one that could result in your exiting the stock through either fear of an even greater loss or hitting your money management risk level or stop loss. Even if you are right in your expectations, if your timing is wrong, you may lose money or make less money than you could have made had your timing been right. Consider your task as an investor to be akin to that of a sharpshooter. Imagine that you are standing with rifle in hand in front of hundreds of moving targets. You have a finite amount of ammunition, and although you may shoot at numerous targets, some are more valuable than others. Furthermore, you may not have many clues about when the targets you wish to shoot will appear. If you open fire at anything that moves, you probably will waste much of your expensive ammunition on minimally valuable targets. The most sensible approach is to wait for valuable targets and shoot them when they appear, conserving your fire power for targets that offer a high reward. Compare this to investors who trade virtually any stock, no matter how potentially valuable, and those who wait patiently for a prime opportunity. There is still another approach. Consider the sharpshooter who studies the behavior of the targets as they pass in front of him and then disappear, only to return again. By patiently observing the pattern made by the targets, the studious sharpshooter will discover when the highly valued targets are likely to appear. As the time period or time window during which these targets are likely to appear approaches, the sharpshooter takes aim and shoots at them repeatedly as they pass in front of him through the window of opportunity, scoring higher points for fewer shots than the individual who shoots at anything that moves and increasing the odds of success by predicting when a valuable target is likely to appear.

Now consider the value of this brief analogy to the task faced by the three basic types of investors. The most common and least successful investor shoots at anything that moves. This individual relies on tips from friends and brokers, on newspaper articles, on the advice of well-known experts, and on instinct. If a stock looks good, it's a buy; if a stock looks bad, or if someone says it's bad, then it must not be worth holding or it may be worth a short sale. Such investors do not consider either the value of trend or the value of their time, money, and effort. Some of them may make money on their haphazard investments, but many lose, and most get into a stock too soon, get out too late, or never get in at all.

The second type of investor is more methodical and recognizes the value of investment capital and the fact that the capital base is finite. This investor doesn't split assets among all manner and sorts of stocks but instead cautiously, even stingily, commits to a few. Patience and persistence are the most valuable tools for this type of investor, who still may not recognize the full value of investing with the major trend. Still, he or she is likely to fare better than the first type of investor because stock picks are biased toward value and in the long run value triumphs and profits are made.

The third type of investor is likely to fare best of all because he or she concentrates on value, patterns, and trend. By studying the relationship of prices and their repetitive patterns this investor is able to know, with a reasonable amount of error, *when valuable stocks are in their optimal buying window and when the time is right to sell them.* In effect, he or she realizes the importance of price trends and is willing to ride the tide. The simple but important truth is that the general trend of stock prices is the single most valuable fact of life in the stock market. In a rising trend investors can buy virtually any stock and make money. In a falling trend most stocks lose value, no matter how solid they may be, and therein resides the value of the cyclical approach to stock investing. Once the approximate time window for a change in major market trend or individual stock trend has been determined, the appropriate actions can be taken during the time window in order to improve timing and invest with the major trend.

An Example of the Time Window

One of the most reliable and well known of all stock market cycles is the approximate four-year cycle. E. R. Dewey[2] has found 3.8- to 4.4-year cycles in such diverse phenomena as cheese consumption, mice plagues, sunspots, pine grosbeak population, lake levels, tree rings, weather, temperature, corporate sales, wheat prices, pig iron prices, and stock prices. The approximate four-year cycle can be observed and identified both visually and mathematically, but it is not a perfect cycle. Chance events affect the operation of any system, and entropy always makes its presence known. Although the traditional understanding of a cycle as a perfectly regular sinusoidal wave is not applicable to most natural cyclical phenomena, there are some general similarities between them.

A perfect sine wave can be generated by an electrical system as long as the speed of the system's rotating coil remains relatively constant. The wave rises to a peak, turns lower, falls to a bottom, and then repeats its form once again. Perhaps this perfect model of a cycle causes nonscientific minds to refrain from applying cycles to economic phenomena. If cycles in stocks and other economic data are much less regular, reliable, and repetitive than they are in purely physical or biological processes—the approximate four-year cycle in stocks may be as long as five years in some cases or as short as three years in other cases—of what practical application can such a cycle be? If the potential degree of error is so large, how can cycles be used effectively to improve investment results?

Let's return to the approximate four-year cycle in stock indices. Figure 2.1 shows this cycle in the Standard & Poor's 500 stock average from the 1940s through 1989. The approximate four-year cycle highs and lows are indicated by a zig zag which also shows the number of

2. Dewey, E. R., *Selected Writings.* (Irvine, Calif.: Foundation for the Study of Cycles, 1974).

FIGURE 2.1 *The Approximate Four-Year Cycle in Standard & Poors 500 From 1940 through 1989 Showing Highs and Lows*

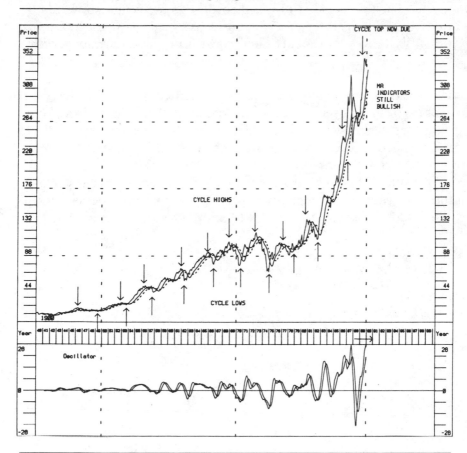

months from low to low. A perfect four-year cycle measures forty-eight months from one low to the next, but some cycles are longer than forty-eight months and some shorter. Most cluster around the forty-eight-month length. The cycles are useful when combined with technical timing indicators. In order to adjust for the inherent inaccuracy of economic cycles a variance is allowed of approximately 10 to 15 percent of the cycle length. A fifty-month cycle, for example, with a 15 percent variance of the cycle length can be as long as 50 + .15 × 50—or 57.5

months, low to low. Allowing the same variance on the early side, a 50-month cycle can be as short as 50 − .15 × 50—or 42.5 months, low to low. The time window (TW), according to my definition, would be from 42.5 months through 57.5 months using a 15% window. During this TW the investor should be looking at prime investment opportunities.

Examine Figures 2.2 and 2.3, which illustrate a model cycle and the way the time between lows and highs is counted. Figure 2.3 illustrates average or mean cycle length. Once length has been determined, compute approximately 10 to 15 percent of the average cycle length, which when added to and subtracted from the average cycle length gives us the approximate time window.

In Figure 2.1—the approximate forty-eight-month cycle in stocks— the time window encompasses a span of about fifteen months, yet the TW could be shortened by using a 10 or even 5 percent period. Further-

FIGURE 2.2 *Schematic Representation of Cycle Lengths*

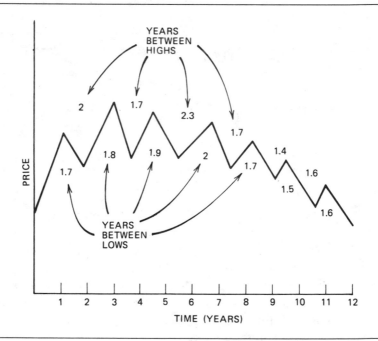

FIGURE 2.3 *Calculating Average Cycle Lengths*

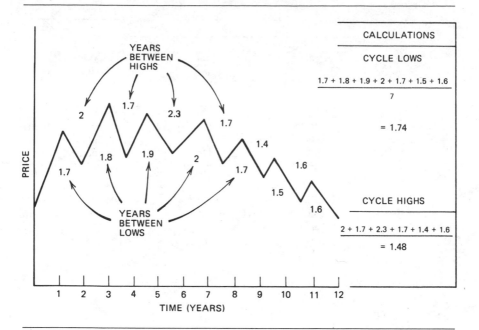

more, applying timing indicators that validate or confirm a probable change in trend can significantly improve the accuracy of the cycles being used. Applying the TW approach to the approximate forty-eight-month cycle in stocks results in the cycles shown in figure 2.4.

Congratulations! You have just completed an analysis of the single most reliable and basic of all stock market cycles. This cycle and the approximate eight- to nine-year cycle (which is its big brother or harmonic) are the two most important cycles for investors to follow. Both are discussed in chapter 3.

As the trend periods in figure 2.4 show, by entering stocks at or near the bottom of the four-year cycles and by exiting stocks at or near the top of the approximate four-year cycles an investor would have participated in virtually every bull market and every bear market since the 1940s. The resulting returns would have been nothing short of phenomenal, provided an investor had the funds, discipline, patience, persistence, and proper individual stock selections. Seems simple, doesn't it?

FIGURE 2.4 *List of Cycle Lengths for the Forty-eight Month S&P Cycle*

Cycle Number	Cycle Starts	Cycle Ends	Cycle Length
1	1953	1957	46 months
2	1957	1962	56 months
3	1962	1966	52 months
4	1966	1970	43 months
5	1970	1974	54 months
6	1974	1978	39 months
7	1978	1982	52 months
8	1982	1987	61 months
9	1987	(Projected 1991)	—
10	—	—	—

Average = 50.38 months

It *is* simple on paper—but very difficult to achieve in reality. On paper we can collapse years and years of prices into lines and numbers and avoid the day-to-day diversions that influence the decision-making processes of investors. Decisions are almost always perfect with the valuable assistance of 20/20 hindsight. "We would have bought here and sold here," we say, examining history with the detached objectivity of scientists. "We would have known that the cyclical top was coming and we would have gotten out." But decisions just aren't made that way. The real world of investing is a place where the best laid plans go astray, a place that tests the mettle of every investor and that daily bombards investors with news, politics, earnings reports, rumors, opinions, innuendoes, and insecurities. The investor who can remain aloof, unaffected, unhampered, unhindered, and uninfluenced by these dysfunctional forces eventually comes out way ahead. In other words, the time window, cycles, and timing can work together as one powerful multifaceted approach, but they are rendered virtually useless by emotion and whimsical actions.

Trends within Trends within Trends

Another factor complicating understanding of cycles is that virtually every cycle is a component of other shorter cycles. The approximate fifty-four-year economic cycle is comprised of two approximate twenty-seven-year cycles. Each twenty-seven-year cycle consists of three nine-year cycles, and each nine-year cycle consists of about two 4.5-year cycles. Finally, each approximate 4.5-year cycle consists of about four to five eleven-month cycles. Figure 2.5 (figure 1.8 in chapter 1) illustrates the general relationship between stock market cycles of various lengths.

FIGURE 2.5 *The Relationship between Cycles of Different Lengths*

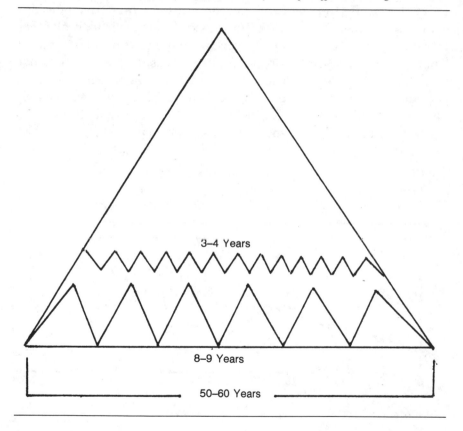

Reexamining this figure now may prove instructive. One caveat, however: This method of representing cycles is theoretical. In practice most cycles cluster around an average cyclical length, and the investor must employ other technical tools in conjunction with cyclical analysis.

As the figure shows, many different cycles operate in a given market at all times. Assume, for example, that three-, five-, eight-, and seventeen-year cycles were all important cycles in a certain market. The final product of all four cyclical components might look something like figure 2.6. However, the market broken into its four cyclical components, each examined individually, might look like figure 2.7. This is why it is often difficult to visualize a given cycle by studying prices in chart form and why cyclical tops and bottoms are often shifted in time.

In other words, cycles interact with one another and in so doing can affect the precise timing of tops and bottoms. Such interrelationships are the rule rather than the exception in stocks and in virtually all other economic phenomena. Although cyclical components may be extracted from a data series using mathematical formulas, this approach is not the best for the individual investor since it is complex and requires considerable effort and expense. Extrapolating the future from a combination or synthesis of cycles, however, is an approach that should interest all investors and speculators. Unfortunately such extrapolations have not achieved an admirable record of success because so many

FIGURE 2.6   *A Combination of Four Cycles: Three, Five, Eight and Seventeen-Year (Dewey and Dakin, 1954), 66.*

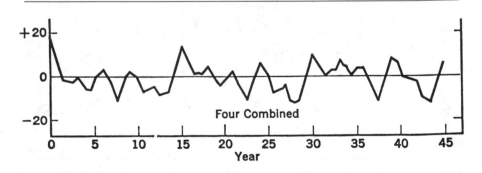

FIGURE 2.7 *How the Four Different Cyclic Components Appear When Broken Out From the Combined Chart (Dewey and Dakin, 1954), 66.*

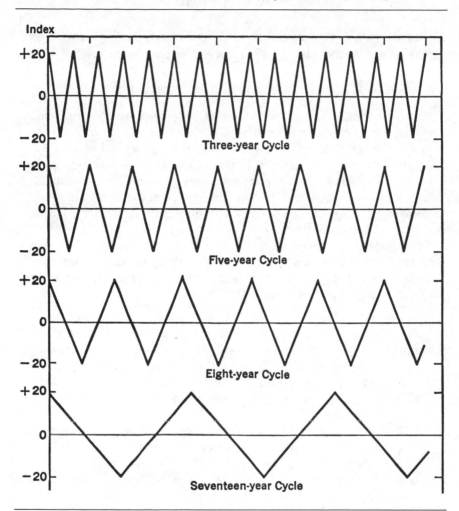

different cyclical factors function at the same time that it is difficult, perhaps impossible, to extract and reconstruct them for the purpose of prediction. This raises the important issue of forecasting or predicting trends as opposed to timing and following trends.

Predicting or Forecasting with Cycles: Which is Best?

The investing and trading public always has been fascinated with forecasts and predictions. In my 1982 book *The Handbook of Commodity Cycles*[3] I discuss the differences between following trends and forecasting trends as they relate to the investor or speculator:

> It took me about nine years to realize that, although it may be a romantic and ego-gratifying goal, forecasting is not necessarily synonymous with profit. The act of determining *where* a market is going and *when* it will get there poses for me and for most traders a distinct *disadvantage* in profitable trading because it predisposes one to particular expectations. Expectations are what lead us to misperceive events, misread indicators, lose confidence in our signals, and avoid implementing decisions that we should know will "work."

What should a trader do? I believe that Joseph Granville, stock market technician supreme, has one answer. The thing to do is simply and exclusively to follow the market, because it is the market we are using as the trading vehicle. Granville (1980) says:

> Following Wall Street analysts will seldom make you money but following a good stock market analyst will. We don't buy and sell the economy. We buy and sell stocks. Why do people forever try to link the economy with the stock market? Economics have nothing to do with stock market timing—and timing is everything. Yet the press will forever clutter up their market commentary with discussions of the economy.[4]
>
>   The first thing to do about the market is get in gear with it. . . . It is never too late to buy stocks as long as the market traffic light is green. That remains true even if you are buying stocks one day before a top. Who cares? You would simply follow the market sell signal, sell everything and then go 100% short across the board. That is called following the market.[5]

In short, it is absolutely necessary to follow the market without attempting to impose upon it any preconceived notions. I believe that a

3. Bernstein, J., *The Handbook of Commodity Cycles*. New York: John Wiley & Sons, 1982).
4. Granville, J., (Kansas City, Mo.: *Stock Market Letter*. 1980), vol. 18, no. 37.
5. Ibid.

market technician can only be a market technician, nothing more, nothing less.[6]

It is not surprising that much of the investment world is preoccupied with the issues of forecasting and predicting. Indeed, I feel that volatile markets and unstable world economies require that investors recognize the need to forecast. In Greek mythology oracles were consulted prior to virtually all major decisions, and many people were dismayed to learn that the Reagans consulted an astrologer. But most people are not reluctant to take a glance at their horoscopes in the daily newspaper, and thousands, perhaps millions, of people throughout the world regularly consult with psychics, clairvoyants, Tarot readers, crystal ball readers, fortune tellers, the I Ching, or tea leaf readers. Despite this human need to know the future, the future is only minimally predictable.

Few individuals have demonstrated an ability to predict the future, regardless of the means they employ—technical or occult. Moreover, it is questionable whether knowledge of the future would guarantee the ability to act on that knowledge.

This book was not written to teach you techniques that allow you to forecast the future but to teach you an investment method that combines expectation with timing.

Cycles in Individual Stocks

Numerous cycles appear in the various stock market averages, but specific stocks also are cyclical and follow cycles in stock averages. The investor who uses cyclical analysis should prioritize his tasks as follows:

1. Track the long-term, intermediate-term, and short-term cycles in stock indices.
2. Monitor stocks that tend to move in conjunction with the stock cycle averages.

---

6. Bernstein (1982), 5.

3. Apply specific market timing indicators to the stock averages and to individual stocks in order to determine when a change in trend is most likely to occur.

4. Take the appropriate action.

Because a rising tide lifts all the boats, your greatest and most important task is to determine trend, trend change, and anticipated trend change in the major stock indices based on cyclical methods discussed in this book.

At this point I would like to stress that it is much more important to know the direction of the stock market in general than the direction of a specific cycle in a specific stock. The strength of the market itself often overrides individual cycles in particular stocks. Even weak stocks in bearish cycles may move higher with a generally rising stock market. Inasmuch as the underlying trend of the stock market in general is measured by various stock averages (such as the Dow Jones industrial average, Dow Jones transportation or utilities averages, Standard & Poor's 100 and 500 stock averages, and Value Line stock average), these averages are comprised of groups of stocks. In some cases the total number of stocks represented is small, as in the Dow Jones industrial average, and in some cases the number of stocks represented is large, as in the Standard & Poor's 500 average or the Value Line average. When many stocks are represented by the averages, most other stocks probably will move in the direction of the broad-based stock averages.

Cycles in particular industry groupings—such as the transportation stock index, the drug stock index, or the electronic stocks index—also should be studied. The study, analysis, and forecasting of trends and cycles in these indices in conjunction with a study of cycles in stock averages will help you determine which stocks you want to include in your portfolio. Select those that are most likely to move with the averages you have selected. Here is where you need to apply a more fundamental analytical approach. Once you have decided which way the market in general is likely to move, and once you have determined that timing indicators support your expectations, study and analyze particular stocks in various industry groups. Examine their price charts and timing indicators and their earnings and prospects for growth. Then make a decision based on the overall weight of the combined evidence.

Other Types of Cyclical Indicators

Although the strict cyclical analyst might disagree with me, I have assigned several other price- and trend-related phenomena to the category of cycles by virtue of their repetitive nature. I included among these decade, day-of-the-week, and preholiday patterns.

Decade Patterns

Some markets and indicators have demonstrated an uncanny pattern of lows and highs at a fairly similar time in each decade. Long-term interest rate yields (bond yields) have shown such a pattern for a hundred years. Bond yields tend to be at their low toward the middle of each decade and at their high point either in the last year of each decade or early in the next decade. This is, in effect, a ten-year cycle. Figures 2.8 and 2.9 illustrate the mid-decade interest rate pattern. Furthermore, consider the pattern in short-term interest rates (such as T-bill yields) as illustrated in figures 2.10 and 2.11.

Day-of-the-Week

In addition to the decade patterns discussed above, markets also exhibit day-of-the-week patterns in relation to closing prices. In other words, specific closing price relationships tend to forecast subsequent closing price behavior with a fairly high degree of accuracy. A study by Yale Hirsch using day-of-the-week patterns yielded some of the results shown in figures 2.12 and 2.13 As you can see, there are certain day-of-the-week patterns for high and low prices in stocks.

Preholiday Behavior

Art Merrill, in his classic book *The Behavior of Prices on Wall Street,*[7] statistically demonstrated the existence of high probability closing price

---

7. Merrill, A., *The Behavior of Prices on Wall Street* (Chappaqua NY: Analysis Press, 1982).

FIGURE 2.8   *The Ten-Year Pattern in T-Bond Yields 1857–1987*

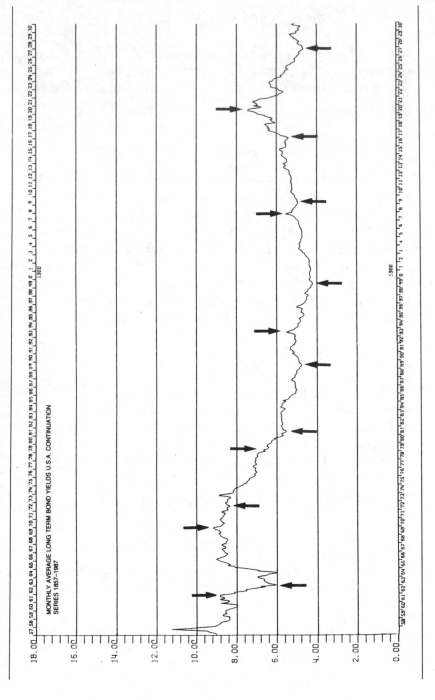

MONTHLY AVERAGE LONG TERM BOND YIELDS U.S.A. CONTINUATION
SERIES 1857–1987

FIGURE 2.8 *Continued*

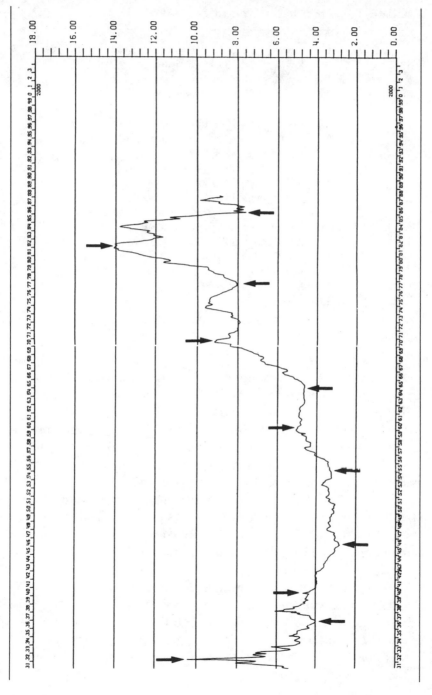

FIGURE 2.9   *The Ten-Year Pattern 1831–1996*

1. 1831 low through 1842 low = eleven years
2. 1842 low through 1852 low = ten years
3. 1852 low through 1863 low = eleven years
4. 1863 low to 1872 low = nine years
5. 1872 low through 1881 low = nine years
6. 1881 low through 1889 low = eight years (actually closer to nine years because of early-1881 low)
7. 1889 low through 1898 low = ten years
8. 1898 low through 1908 low = nine years
9. 1908 low through 1916 low = eight years
10. 1916 low through 1927 low = eleven years
11. 1927 low through 1936 low = nine years
12. 1936 low through 1946 low = ten years
13. 1946 low through 1954 low = eight years
14. 1954 low through 1965 low = eleven years
15. 1965 low through 1977 low = twelve years
16. 1977 low through 1986 low = nine years
17. 1986 low through projected 1996 low = ten years

patterns in the Dow Jones industrial averages. Figure 2.14 shows some of Merrill's statistical findings regarding the preholiday behavior of stock prices.

As you can see from the Merrill statistical studies, the importance of pre-holiday behavior cannot be underestimated. Veteran investors and speculators should be familiar with these patterns. There is yet another important consideration of pre-holiday behavior. When the market fails to act in a fashion consistent with pre-holiday behavior, investors should consider it a warning sign that all may not be well with the market. This is also an important consideration in all seasonal price behavior of which pre-holiday behavior is only a small aspect.

As a speculator or short term trader you can use pre-holiday behavior to your advantage by entering the stock market at the close of trading on the day before a high probability date. For example, if you know that stock prices tend to close higher on the business day before Christmas, you could use this information to your advantage.

FIGURE 2.10   *The Decade Pattern in T-Bill Yields. Arrows down (↓) show late decade tops and letters A Through G show early decade low pattern.*

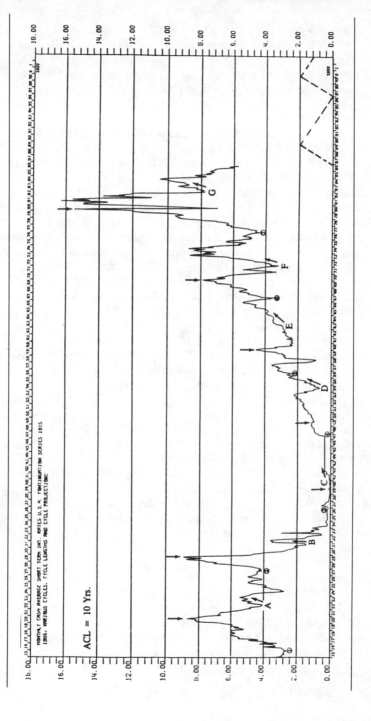

FIGURE 2.11 *Analysis of Early Decade Low Pattern in T-Bill Yield*

1. A low was made in 1830, consistent with the early-decade-low pattern. This was followed by an upswing that brought commercial paper rates from a low of 6 percent to a high of more than 18 percent during the next five years. In this case, the early-decade low coincided with the approximate ten-year cycle low.
2. Another low was made in 1841, again coinciding with the approximate ten-year cycle low.
3. Another low was made in 1851. It brought commercial paper rates from a low in the 6½ percent area to a high in the 12¾ percent area. Once again the importance of early-decade lows is plain to see.
4. A low was made in approximately 1862—again, early in the decade. This low marked the start of a slow but certain rise in rates from approximately 5½ percent to a high of 9¾ percent.
5. This was followed by a low in the 1871 time frame. Although rates moved higher, they stopped their ascent about one year after their bottom.
6. A low was made in 1883, again relatively early in the new decade; however, it was not a significant low in terms of appreciation inasmuch as interest rates climbed only briefly before turning lower again.
7. Another low was made in the 1883–84 time frame, still in the early part of the decade but later than had been the case since the 1831 bottom. It appeared as if the early-decade-low pattern was beginning to fail.
8. Another low was made in early 1894, still in the first half of the decade but not as early as had been the case in the 1830–71 time frame.
9. The next low came in the late 1903/early 1904 time frame. It appeared as if the early-decade-low pattern was beginning to take hold again.
10. Then from late 1930 to early 1931, interest rates made a low that failed to last. Another attempt at a low was made in 1932. From 1932 through 1940 a sideways-to-lower pattern developed that eventually brought prices down to their early-decade low in 1940. Now the pattern was back on schedule.
11. The next low was actually made in 1954; however, the 1950–51 time frame was a level from which rates moved higher for several years. In fact, the 1954 low was not much lower than the 1950 low. The validity of early-decade lows in short-term interest rates was maintained.
12. There could not have been a more perfect validation of this pattern than the bottoming phase in short-term interest rates that developed from 1960 to 1961. Again, the validity of short-term interest rate lows early in the decade was confirmed.
13. Short-term interest rates "took off" only to peak in the late 1960s. This was followed by another early-decade low. This time the bottom came in the 1970–72 time frame. Thereafter, short-term interest rates jumped sharply for several years, peaking in the 1974 time frame.
14. Then, in early 1980, interest rates bottomed again, consistent with the early-decade-low pattern, and skyrocketed to all-time highs in 1981, only to begin a steady and fairly persistent decline to the approximate ten-year cycle low in 1986.

FIGURE 2.12 *Daily Market Probability Calendar (Hirsch, 1986, p. 117)*

Date	Jan.	Feb.	Mar.	Apr.	May	June	July	Aug.	Sept.	Oct.	Nov.	Dec.
1	H	SAT	SAT	63.6	50.0	SUN	63.6	54.5	H	39.4	SAT	45.4
2	48.4	SUN	SUN	48.4	73.5	52.9	66.7	SAT	66.7	75.8	SUN	48.4
3	75.8	57.6	72.7	51.5	SAT	52.9	63.6	SUN	63.6	57.6	60.6	63.6
4	SAT	57.6	63.6	51.5	SUN	58.8	H	42.4	63.6	SAT	60.6	69.7
5	SUN	39.4	57.6	SAT	64.7	64.7	SAT	51.5	45.4	SUN	75.8	45.4
6	54.5	48.4	48.4	SUN	52.9	52.9	SUN	57.6	SAT	66.7	48.4	SAT
7	51.5	48.4	42.4	63.6	55.9	SAT	60.6	60.6	SUN	57.6	45.4	SUN
8	42.4	SAT	SAT	60.6	50.0	SUN	60.6	36.4	45.4	51.5	SAT	48.4
9	48.4	SUN	SUN	69.7	41.2	50.0	60.6	SAT	48.4	45.4	SUN	57.6
10	51.5	36.4	54.5	54.5	SAT	32.4	42.4	SUN	48.4	42.4	57.6	48.4
11	SAT	39.4	66.7	54.5	SUN	64.7	30.3	57.6	60.6	SAT	72.7	45.4
12	SUN	57.6	54.5	SAT	47.1	58.8	SAT	45.4	45.4	SUN	60.6	51.5
13	51.5	45.4	60.6	SUN	35.3	50.0	SUN	54.5	SAT	39.4	48.4	SAT
14	63.6	45.4	42.4	57.6	44.1	SAT	63.6	57.6	SUN	39.4	45.4	SUN
15	57.6	SAT	SAT	54.5	47.1	SUN	54.5	54.5	54.5	39.4	SAT	54.5
16	42.4	SUN	SUN	54.5	50.0	52.9	36.4	SAT	48.4	57.6	SUN	54.5
17	54.5	H	54.5	57.6	SAT	47.1	45.4	SUN	51.5	45.4	60.6	45.4
18	SAT	39.4	63.6	51.5	SUN	47.1	39.4	45.4	45.4	SAT	51.5	48.4
19	SUN	42.4	57.6	SAT	32.4	52.9	SAT	45.4	54.5	SUN	69.7	48.4
20	54.5	48.4	45.4	SUN	44.1	50.0	SUN	54.5	SAT	57.6	66.7	SAT
21	45.4	54.5	45.4	45.4	50.0	SAT	48.4	39.4	SUN	48.4	54.5	SUN
22	51.5	SAT	SAT	54.5	50.0	SUN	51.5	42.4	54.5	36.4	SAT	48.4
23	69.7	SUN	SUN	39.4	44.1	50.0	48.4	SAT	51.5	33.3	SUN	36.4
24	60.6	30.3	54.5	57.6	SAT	38.2	42.4	SUN	54.5	51.5	72.7	63.6
25	SAT	42.4	33.3	63.6	SUN	47.1	45.4	45.4	54.5	SAT	54.5	H
26	SUN	57.6	51.5	SAT	H	52.9	SAT	33.3	57.6	SUN	54.5	69.7
27	39.4	45.4	54.5	SUN	41.2	52.9	SUN	51.5	SAT	30.3	H	SAT
28	57.6	57.6	H	39.4	32.4	SAT	54.5	51.5	SUN	54.5	54.5	SUN
29	39.4	—	SAT	39.4	52.9	SUN	54.5	75.8	39.4	57.6	SAT	51.5
30	63.6	—	SUN	57.6	58.8	58.8	57.6	SAT	33.3	45.4	SUN	63.6
31	60.6	—	36.4	—	SAT	—	63.6	SUN	—	48.4	—	78.8

1. Buy one of the Blue Chip or Dow Industrial stocks on the close of trading the day before the key date. You will be betting that the statistical validity will be maintained and that the Dow Jones Industrial Average (DJIA) will close higher the next day. If this does in fact occur, then you would close out your position on or immediately prior to the close of trading the next day.

2. You could trade the OEX index stock option according to the plan discussed in item 1 above. This would entail more risk since you would be buying an option based on a broad market index.

FIGURE 2.13 *Market Performance Each Day of the Month (Hirsch, 1986, p. 30)*

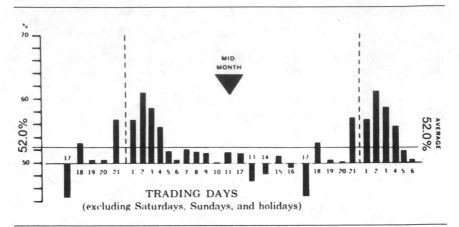

TRADING DAYS
(excluding Saturdays, Sundays, and holidays)

However, the odds of your OEX option moving with the general market would be considerably greater than the odds of an upmove in one stock.

3. If you are a long term investor who is interested in closing out some of your stocks, you could wait for one of the pre-holiday high probability days and exit your stocks toward the end of trading on that day.

4. If you are bearish on stocks, you could take advantage of a possible rally by selling short on or near the close of trading.

If you use pre-holiday price behavior of the DJIA you should keep up to date on its statistical performance. Figure 2.15 shows the percentage of time the DJIA has closed higher or lower for the periods surrounding Independence Day, Christmas Day and New Year's Day.

You might ask whether pre-holiday behavior will continue to be valid given the fact that so many investors and traders know about it. Based on the high degree of statistical validity associated with these dates, I suspect that they are likely to continue to be valid. You might also ask whether there are other reliable up or down days of the year in the DJIA. To answer this question see Figure 2.16 which shows the percentage of times prices have closed up or down in the DJIA since the 1940s. As you can see, there are both high probability up days and high probability down days.

FIGURE 2.14 *Pre- and Post Holiday Behavior of the Dow Jones Industrial Average (Merrill, 1982)*

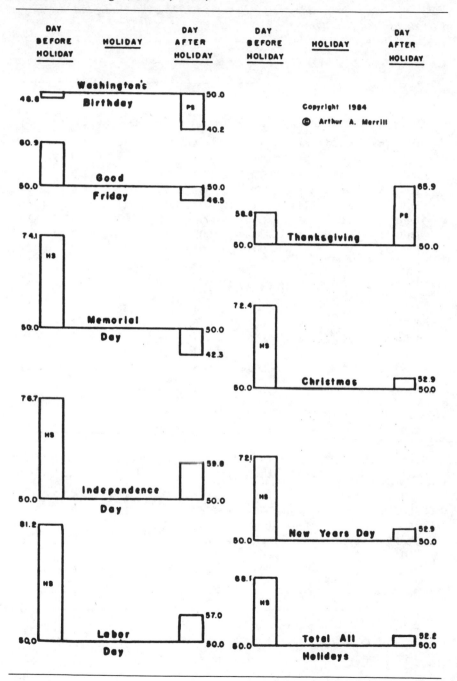

FIGURE 2.15   *Pre-holiday DJIA Behavior 1947–1990 (Independence Day, Christmas, and New Year's)*

Christmas and New Year's

Month/ Day	% Up	% Down	Average Up	Average Down	Years Up	Years Down	Years Unch	Total
DEC 15	45	54	.005	−.005	16	19	0	35
+DEC 16	61	38	.007	−.005	21	13	0	34
DEC 17	50	50	.006	−.007	17	17	0	34
+DEC 18	66	33	.008	−.007	22	11	0	33
+DEC 19	61	38	.005	−.004	21	13	0	34
−DEC 20	32	67	.005	−.005	11	23	0	34
DEC 21	45	54	.006	−.003	16	19	0	35
DEC 22	57	42	.006	−.004	20	15	0	35
DEC 23	44	55	.004	−.005	15	19	0	34
++DEC 24	74	25	.005	−.003	20	7	0	27
+DEC 26	69	30	.007	−.005	18	8	0	26
DEC 27	47	52	.009	−.004	16	18	0	34
DEC 28	50	47	.004	−.006	17	16	1	34
DEC 29	51	48	.006	−.004	18	17	0	35
+DEC 30	61	35	.006	−.004	21	12	1	34
+DEC 31	64	32	.005	−.003	22	11	1	34

Independence Day

Month/ Day	% Up	% Down	Average Up	Average Down	Years Up	Years Down	Years Unch	Total
+JUL 1	64	32	.005	−.005	22	11	1	34
+JUL 2	64	35	.006	−.006	22	12	0	34
++JUL 3	75	24	.006	−.003	22	7	0	29
+JUL 5	69	30	.006	−.007	18	8	0	26
JUL 6	57	42	.007	−.006	20	15	0	35
JUL 7	51	48	.005	−.007	18	17	0	35

FIGURE 2.16 *Percentage of Times DJIA Prices Close Up or Down, Every Calendar Date, July–December, 1940–1990*

Month/	%		Average		Years			
Day	Up	Down	Up	Down	Up	Down	Unch	Total
+JUL 1	66	31	.007	−.005	44	21	1	66
+JUL 2	60	39	.006	−.006	40	26	0	66
++JUL 3	70	27	.008	−.004	43	17	1	61
+JUL 5	62	37	.008	−.010	32	19	0	51
+JUL 6	62	37	.009	−.005	41	25	0	66
JUL 7	53	46	.005	−.009	35	31	0	66
JUL 8	57	42	.006	−.007	38	28	0	66
JUL 9	50	50	.007	−.005	33	33	0	66
JUL 10	47	50	.007	−.007	31	33	1	65
JUL 11	47	52	.007	−.007	31	34	0	65
JUL 12	50	47	.008	−.008	33	31	1	65
−JUL 13	39	60	.008	−.006	26	40	0	66
+JUL 14	67	32	.006	−.007	44	21	0	65
JUL 15	50	50	.005	−.007	33	33	0	66
JUL 16	57	40	.007	−.005	38	27	1	66
JUL 17	56	41	.008	−.006	37	27	1	65
JUL 18	53	44	.007	−.006	35	29	1	65
JUL 19	56	43	.007	−.007	37	28	0	65
JUL 20	54	43	.008	−.009	36	29	1	66
JUL 21	43	56	.007	−.010	28	37	0	65
JUL 22	54	45	.007	−.007	36	30	0	66
JUL 23	57	42	.005	−.007	38	28	0	66
−JUL 24	38	61	.008	−.006	25	40	0	65
JUL 25	56	43	.008	−.007	37	28	0	65
+JUL 26	64	35	.005	−.011	42	23	0	65
+JUL 27	60	36	.008	−.008	40	24	2	66
JUL 28	53	46	.009	−.007	35	31	0	66
JUL 29	46	53	.007	−.009	31	35	0	66
JUL 30	56	43	.006	−.008	37	29	0	66
JUL 31	54	45	.007	−.007	35	29	0	64
AUG 1	55	44	.008	−.006	36	29	0	65
AUG 2	59	40	.008	−.007	38	26	0	64
AUG 3	53	44	.009	−.005	34	28	1	63
AUG 4	52	47	.006	−.008	34	31	0	65
AUG 5	41	58	.007	−.007	27	38	0	65
AUG 6	47	49	.007	−.007	31	32	2	65
AUG 7	54	45	.007	−.006	35	29	0	64
AUG 8	49	50	.008	−.008	32	33	0	65

FIGURE 2.16 (*Continued*)

Month/	%		Average		Years			
Day	Up	Down	Up	Down	Up	Down	Unch	Total
AUG 9	40	58	.009	−.007	26	38	1	65
AUG 10	46	51	.006	−.008	30	33	1	64
AUG 11	53	46	.008	−.006	35	30	0	65
AUG 12	50	49	.009	−.011	33	32	0	65
+AUG 13	66	32	.007	−.010	43	21	1	65
AUG 14	56	43	.006	−.008	36	28	0	64
AUG 15	57	40	.009	−.005	37	26	1	64
AUG 16	57	42	.009	−.007	37	27	0	64
+AUG 17	60	40	.009	−.006	39	26	0	65
AUG 18	49	49	.004	−.008	32	32	1	65
AUG 19	39	59	.006	−.008	25	38	1	64
+AUG 20	61	38	.007	−.007	40	25	0	65
AUG 21	45	53	.008	−.008	29	34	1	64
AUG 22	52	47	.009	−.006	34	31	0	65
AUG 23	49	50	.009	−.009	32	33	0	65
AUG 24	49	50	.009	−.007	32	33	0	65
AUG 25	47	50	.006	−.006	31	33	1	65
+AUG 26	61	38	.006	−.007	40	25	0	65
AUG 27	50	49	.007	−.008	33	32	0	65
AUG 28	50	50	.006	−.005	32	32	0	64
+AUG 29	60	36	.007	−.007	39	24	2	65
AUG 30	46	53	.008	−.005	30	35	0	65
AUG 31	55	44	.005	−.007	35	28	0	63
+SEP 1	61	38	.006	−.009	32	20	0	52
SEP 2	59	38	.009	−.007	31	20	1	52
SEP 3	53	46	.008	−.011	28	24	0	52
SEP 4	43	56	.007	−.008	23	30	0	53
SEP 5	54	45	.013	−.007	29	24	0	53
SEP 6	55	44	.008	−.007	29	23	0	52
SEP 7	59	40	.005	−.008	31	21	0	52
SEP 8	46	53	.005	−.007	30	35	0	65
SEP 9	47	52	.006	−.009	31	34	0	65
SEP 10	42	57	.006	−.010	27	37	0	64
SEP 11	47	50	.009	−.007	31	33	1	65
SEP 12	47	52	.006	−.008	31	34	0	65
SEP 13	42	57	.008	−.009	27	37	0	64
SEP 14	48	51	.007	−.010	31	33	0	64
SEP 15	49	50	.007	−.008	32	33	0	65
+SEP 16	64	33	.007	−.007	42	22	1	65

Month/ Day	%		Average		Years			
	Up	Down	Up	Down	Up	Down	Unch	Total
SEP 17	55	43	.007	−.008	36	28	1	65
SEP 18	50	49	.006	−.010	33	32	0	65
SEP 19	43	53	.009	−.009	28	35	2	65
SEP 20	48	51	.008	−.009	31	33	0	64
SEP 21	50	48	.011	−.010	32	31	1	64
SEP 22	49	50	.007	−.007	32	33	0	65
SEP 23	49	49	.009	−.009	32	32	1	65
SEP 24	52	46	.006	−.011	34	30	1	65
SEP 25	44	55	.006	−.008	29	36	0	65
SEP 26	46	51	.005	−.010	31	34	1	66
SEP 27	47	50	.008	−.009	30	32	1	63
SEP 28	48	51	.009	−.009	31	33	0	64
SEP 29	47	52	.007	−.009	31	34	0	65
SEP 30	49	49	.008	−.008	32	32	1	65
+OCT 1	61	36	.008	−.007	40	24	1	65
+OCT 2	65	32	.007	−.006	42	21	1	64
OCT 3	52	47	.008	−.008	34	31	0	65
OCT 4	46	53	.008	−.006	30	35	0	65
+OCT 5	62	37	.007	−.016	40	24	0	64
OCT 6	53	45	.012	−.009	34	29	1	64
OCT 7	49	49	.010	−.007	32	32	1	65
OCT 8	43	56	.009	−.008	28	37	0	65
OCT 9	48	51	.007	−.010	31	33	0	64
OCT 10	53	46	.009	−.010	35	30	0	65
OCT 11	56	43	.009	−.009	37	28	0	65
−OCT 12	35	61	.012	−.007	12	21	1	34
OCT 13	48	51	.009	−.010	28	30	0	58
OCT 14	44	55	.011	−.010	29	36	0	65
OCT 15	56	43	.008	−.009	37	28	0	65
OCT 16	46	53	.011	−.011	30	34	0	64
OCT 17	53	46	.007	−.007	35	30	0	65
OCT 18	56	43	.007	−.009	37	28	0	65
OCT 19	44	55	.006	−.016	29	36	0	65
++OCT 20	72	27	.012	−.007	47	18	0	65
OCT 21	46	52	.011	−.008	30	34	1	65
−OCT 22	38	61	.007	−.009	25	40	0	65
OCT 23	45	53	.008	−.010	29	34	1	64
OCT 24	44	49	.008	−.005	29	32	4	65
−OCT 25	36	63	.006	−.006	24	41	0	65
−OCT 26	36	63	.007	−.009	24	41	0	65
OCT 27	46	52	.008	−.007	30	34	1	65

FIGURE 2.16 (*Continued*)

Month/	%		Average		Years			
Day	Up	Down	Up	Down	Up	Down	Unch	Total
OCT 28	45	54	.007	−.011	29	35	0	64
OCT 29	50	50	.009	−.010	32	32	0	64
OCT 30	54	42	.012	−.009	35	27	2	64
OCT 31	50	49	.010	−.008	33	32	0	65
+NOV 1	65	34	.008	−.008	41	22	0	63
+NOV 2	62	37	.008	−.009	34	20	0	54
+NOV 3	64	35	.011	−.010	36	20	0	56
NOV 4	50	49	.011	−.007	28	27	0	55
NOV 5	59	40	.008	−.012	32	22	0	54
NOV 6	48	51	.008	−.014	27	29	0	56
NOV 7	56	43	.012	−.008	31	24	0	55
NOV 8	42	55	.008	−.010	23	30	1	54
NOV 9	54	43	.011	−.011	35	28	1	64
NOV 10	50	47	.010	−.010	33	31	1	65
+NOV 11	68	31	.010	−.015	33	15	0	48
NOV 12	53	45	.009	−.011	33	28	1	62
−NOV 13	37	60	.007	−.010	25	40	1	66
NOV 14	53	46	.010	−.009	35	31	0	66
NOV 15	54	43	.008	−.007	35	28	1	64
NOV 16	56	43	.008	−.009	36	28	0	64
NOV 17	58	41	.006	−.006	38	27	0	65
NOV 18	43	55	.009	−.009	28	36	1	65
NOV 19	47	52	.007	−.009	31	34	0	65
NOV 20	59	40	.008	−.007	38	26	0	64
NOV 21	49	50	.009	−.006	32	33	0	65
NOV 22	46	53	.009	−.009	27	31	0	58
NOV 23	52	47	.005	−.010	29	26	0	55
NOV 24	54	43	.008	−.008	28	22	1	51
NOV 25	56	44	.005	−.010	28	22	0	50
+NOV 26	62	37	.011	−.010	33	20	0	53
NOV 27	59	40	.009	−.009	32	22	0	54
NOV 28	48	51	.007	−.010	26	28	0	54
NOV 29	45	54	.009	−.006	26	31	0	57
NOV 30	42	55	.009	−.008	25	33	1	59
DEC 1	57	42	.007	−.008	36	27	0	63
DEC 2	57	42	.008	−.010	36	27	0	63
DEC 3	58	41	.008	−.008	37	26	0	63
+DEC 4	60	38	.007	−.008	38	24	1	63
DEC 5	50	49	.007	−.007	33	32	0	65

Month/	%		Average		Years			
Day	Up	Down	Up	Down	Up	Down	Unch	Total
DEC 6	54	45	.010	−.007	35	29	0	64
DEC 7	53	44	.008	−.007	34	28	1	63
DEC 8	46	53	.006	−.008	29	34	0	63
DEC 9	53	44	.007	−.009	34	28	1	63
DEC 10	53	46	.006	−.010	34	29	0	63
DEC 11	44	55	.006	−.008	28	35	0	63
DEC 12	44	55	.005	−.010	29	36	0	65
DEC 13	51	48	.006	−.007	33	31	0	64
DEC 14	58	41	.009	−.008	37	26	0	63
DEC 15	46	53	.005	−.007	30	34	0	64
DEC 16	53	46	.007	−.008	34	30	0	64
DEC 17	51	48	.007	−.008	33	31	0	64
DEC 18	53	45	.011	−.008	34	29	1	64
DEC 19	56	43	.006	−.006	37	28	0	65
DEC 20	43	54	.006	−.008	28	35	1	64
DEC 21	42	57	.007	−.007	27	37	0	64
DEC 22	54	45	.009	−.007	35	29	0	64
DEC 23	48	51	.006	−.007	31	33	0	64
++DEC 24	73	26	.005	−.006	41	15	0	56
+DEC 26	64	35	.009	−.007	33	18	0	51
DEC 27	48	51	.010	−.006	31	33	0	64
DEC 28	52	46	.009	−.008	33	29	1	63
+DEC 29	60	39	.007	−.005	39	25	0	64
+DEC 30	62	35	.008	−.004	40	23	1	64
++DEC 31	73	25	.008	−.003	47	16	1	64

Chapter 3

Examining Some Long-Term Stock Cycles

There are no definitive rules for the classification of cyclical lengths. What is long term to one investor is short term to another. The following list reflects my own bias:

Long-term cycles are approximately one year or longer from one low point to the next.

Intermediate-term cycles are approximately three months to one year in length from one low point to the next.

Short-term cycles have an average length of less than three months from one low point to the next.

This chapter will examine some long-term stock cycles. The next two chapters examine intermediate- and short-term cycles, respectively, and draw on a variety of historical studies published by the Foundation for the Study of Cycles.

The Catalogue of Cycles Part I by Louise L. Wilson[1] lists alleged cycles in the stock market ranging from 20 hours to 89 ½ years. Because this chapter is concerned only with a discussion of the long-term cycles in stocks according to the definition provided above, it examines cycles of one year in length or longer. I first illustrate and investigate the validity of such cycles in the various stock indices (the Dow Jones industrial average and the Standard & Poor's 500 stock average) and then explore similar cycles in individual stocks.

---

1. Wilson, L., *The Catalogue of Cycles Part I* (Irvine, Calif.: Foundation for the Study of Cycles).

Numerous long-term cycles have been alleged to exist in stock prices—enough, in fact, so that exploring the validity of each would fill an entire book. I therefore focus only on those that I feel are sufficiently reliable to be valuable to stock investors.

In 1972 Dewey and Dakin in their book *Cycles: The Science of Prediction*[2] discussed the predominant long-term stock market cycles. Their focus was primarily on long-term stock cycles and specifically on the approximate fifty-four-year, eighteen-year, nine-year, and 3.5-year cycles.

The Fifty-four-Year Cycle

The name most closely associated with the approximate fifty-four-year cycle is Kondratieff. In fact, the fifty- to sixty-year economic cycle is usually referred to as the Kondratieff wave. Although economist Joseph Schumpeter referred to the Kondratieff wave as the "single most important tool in economic forecasting,"[3] the fifty- to sixty-year cycle and the theories of Kondratieff have been enveloped in controversy since they were first proposed in the 1920s beginning with Kondratieff's banishment to a Siberian labor camp. Communists rejected Kondratieff's hypothesis that capitalist economies fluctuated in cyclical patterns from inflation to deflation because Marxist doctrine preached the eventual collapse of capitalist economies by a workers' revolution.

Another reason for the controversy enveloping the fifty- to sixty-year Kondratieff cycle is the fact that limited statistics are available to validate its existence. Many eminent economists and statisticians doubt the existence of Kondratieff's cycle, yet others, including Jay Forrester of the Massachusetts Institute of Technology Systems Dynamics Group, have amassed hard statistical evidence supporting the long-wave, or fifty- to sixty-year cycle. The Foundation for the Study of Cycles, founded by E. R. Dewey, also has accumulated considerable evidence in support of long-wave cycles.

Yet despite the evidence supporting long waves, the controversy

2. Dewey, Edward R., and Edwin F. Dakin. *Cycles: The Science of Prediction.* New York: Henry Holt & Co., 1947.
3. Schumpeter, Joseph A. *The History of Economic Development.* New York: Oxford University Press, 1954.

continues and the disbelievers are many. Indeed, adherents of Keynesian economics have good reason to doubt the existence of any cycle. Their theories are based on the ability of governments to virtually eliminate the downward portion of any economic trend by expansion and contraction of money supply. My book *The New Prosperity*[4] provides not only the statistical evidence supporting these long-wave cycles but also their social, political, and historical dimensions.

I feel that there is ample statistical evidence supporting the long wave economic cycles. At worst, I'd consider the evidence on both sides to be about equal. Figures 3.1 through 3.4 show the behavior of monthly average stock prices over the last two hundred years.

The figures have been divided to highlight individual cycles. Because stock prices two hundred years ago were much lower than today's prices, a continuous price graph would obscure early price behavior.

The Approximate Nine-Year Cycle

Although an approximate fifty- to sixty-year cycle in stock prices is a fascinating idea indeed, it is supported by relatively little data. This is not so with the approximate eight- to nine-year cycle in stock prices. There have been sufficient repetitions of this cycle to support its statistical validity. E. R. Dewey and others have documented the existence of the approximate eight- to nine-year cycle in numerous articles and studies in *Cycles,* the official publication of the Foundation of the Study of Cycles.[5]

Figure 3.5 shows the approximate eight- to nine-year cycle lows and highs since 1940. As you can see, some of the largest up and down moves in the history of stock prices have occurred during these cycles. As you can see, this cycle has averaged from eight to nine years in length, with some cycles longer or shorter than average.

Although this cycle accounts for many significant rallies and declines in the stock market, it nevertheless has shown considerable variation in length. A strictly cyclical approach to stock market entry and exit using the eight- to nine-year cycle as a reference is not recommended.

---

4. Bernstein, J., *The New Prosperity* (New York: Institute of Finance 1989).
5. *Cycles* published by the Foundation for the Study of Cycles, 124 S. Highland Pittsburgh PA.

FIGURE 3.1 *The 50–60 Year Stock Cycle 1790–1845*

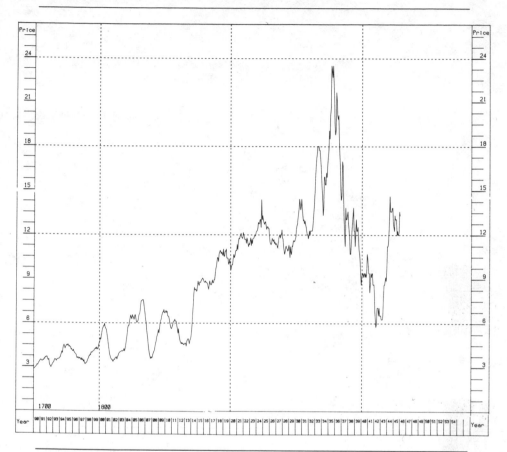

To purchase or sell stocks in expectation of a cyclical turn might result in market entry substantially earlier than would be indicated by actual events. This cycle (and all others) should be used in conjunction with the specific timing indicators discussed in chapter 8.

The approximate eight- to nine-year cycle also can be observed in individual stock prices. Many large moves in stocks are part of the eight- to nine-year cycles. Timing in conjunction with these cycles is essential. When a stock is likely to bottom on its eight- to nine-year cycle, the upward penetration of a resistance trend line is an indication that the low has been made. When a stock is in its eight- to nine-year time window top, the downward penetration of a support trend line is

FIGURE 3.2 *The 50–60 Year Cycle in Stocks 1845–1900*

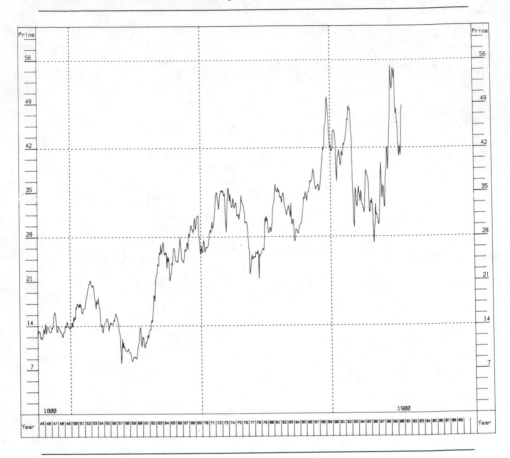

considered evidence that a top has, in fact, been made. The more thorough application of trend line analysis in conjunction with cycles is discussed in greater detail in chapter 8.

The Approximate Three- to Four-Year Cycles

Another cycle of considerable importance in stock prices and in the economy as a whole is the approximate three- to four-year cycle.

FIGURE 3.3 *Approximate 50–60 Year Cycle in Stocks 1900–1955*

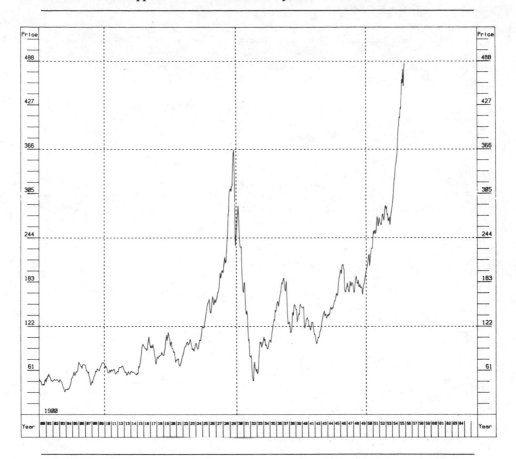

This cycle also occurs in stocks, interest rates, and business and is the cornerstone of variations in capitalist economy business trends. Figures 1.6 and 1.7 have already illustrated some of Kitchin's original research and findings. As evidence of this cycle's value in business note figure 3.7, which illustrates the approximate three- to four-year cycle lows and highs in the Commodity Research Bureau's futures price index.

FIGURE 3.4 *Approximate 50–60 Year Cycle in Stocks 1955–1989 Showing Projected Low*

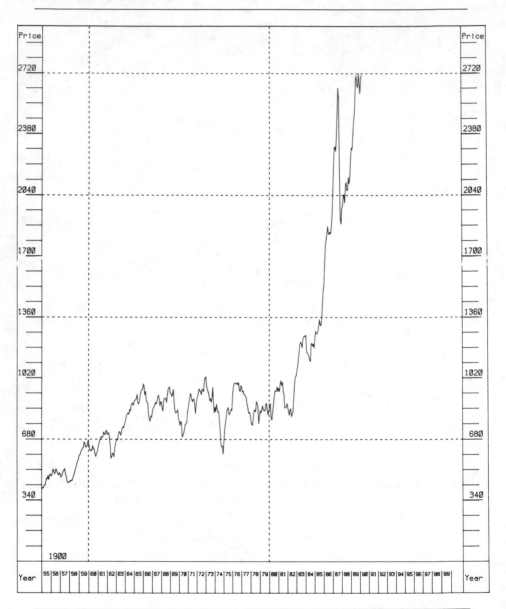

FIGURE 3.5 *The Approximate 9-Year Cycle Lows in Stocks 1940–1991*

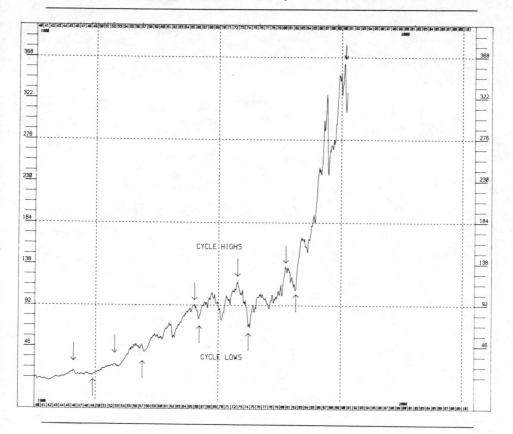

FIGURE 3.6 *The Approximate Three to Four Year Cycle in Interest Rates*

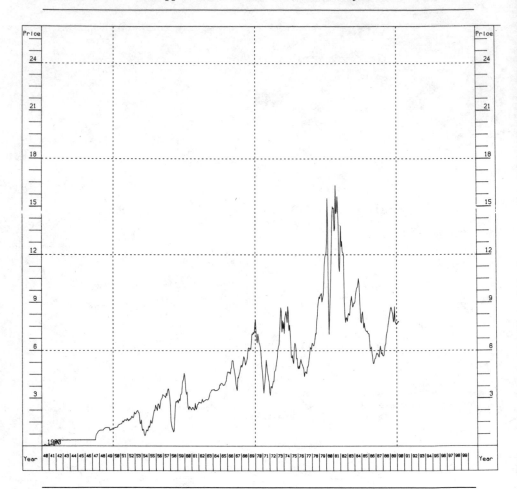

FIGURE 3.7 *The Approximate Three to Four Year Cycle in CRB Index*

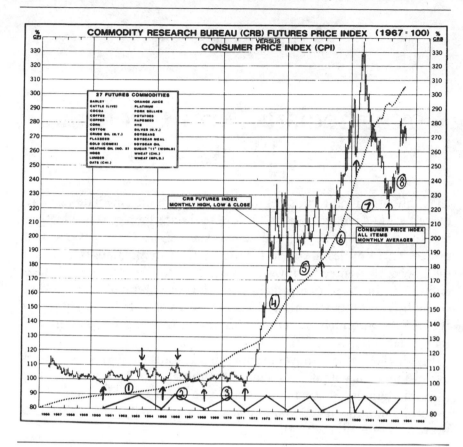

Chapter 4

Intermediate-Term Cycles in Stocks

In addition to long-term stock cycles, there are intermediate-term cycles as well. Among these are the approximate fourteen- to nineteen-week cycles and the approximate twenty-eight- to thirty-six-week cycles. These cycles are ideal for use by the intermediate-term trader but may not be suited for investors other than for the purpose of market entry. The fourteen- to nineteen-week cycle has been researched extensively by the Foundation for the Study of Cycles. It is clearly one of the premier intermediate-term cycles in the stock market, as well as in individual stocks.

Figures 4.1 and 4.2 show the approximate fourteen- to nineteen-week cycles in various stock averages. The timing indicators are discussed fully in chapters 8, 9, and 11. Once you have read the chapters on cyclical timing, I suggest you return to chapter 4 and review the indications in connection with the cycles.

The Importance of Intermediate Term Cycles

Long term and intermediate term cycles are the most important cycles for investors to follow. Of these, the fourteen to nineteen week cycle in stocks is not only the most reliable and predictable, but also the most potentially profitable. Not only is this cycle easily identified, but it is also a cycle which has been reliable for over sixty years. Following are a few suggestions for using the fourteen to nineteen week cycle.

FIGURE 4.1 *The 14–19 Week Cycle in Standard & Poor's Cash Index*

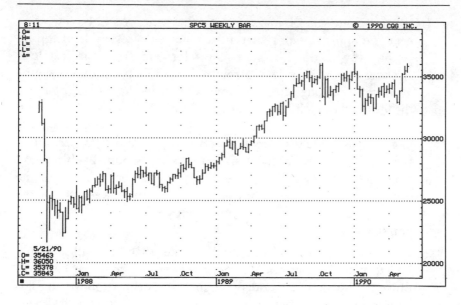

FIGURE 4.2 *The 14–19 Week Cycle in the Dow Jones Transportation Index*

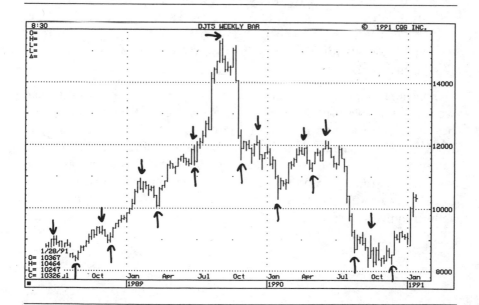

Chart Courtesy of Commodity Quote Graphics

1. When buying stocks, make certain that you are not buying at or
    near the approximate fourteen to nineteen week cyclical top. A
    simple way to do this is to count forward from the last low.
    Assume that this cycle is a relatively symmetrical one. Assume
    also that in a long term bull market (i.e. in the bullish phase of
    the four and or eight year cycles) and that the fourteen to nineteen
    week cycle will be skewed to the right (i.e. late tops). A reasonable
    figure to use would be about twelve weeks (about 75 percent of
    the average cycle length of sixteen weeks). Count twelve weeks
    from the last low and assume that you are near the top of the
    cycle. If you find that it has been about sixteen weeks from the
    last low, then you would conclude that you are buying near a low
    point.

2. If you plan to sell stocks in a bull market then you will probably
    realize your best prices about twelve weeks from the last low,
    utilizing the same general procedure as outlined above. In this
    case, however, you will want to sell on about the twelfth week
    from the last bottom.

3. If you are bearish on stocks in a bear market then you can assume
    that the fourteen to nineteen week cycle tops will be early, usually
    about 25 percent from the previous low. 25 percent of the cycle
    translates into approximately four weeks. You would, therefore,
    begin selling short on about the fourth week from the last bottom,
    and you would want to cover short positions on about the six-
    teenth week from the last bottom.

The intermediate term cycle of approximately fourteen to nineteen
weeks, low to low, will not necessarily be visible in all stocks, but it will
be identified in a good majority of active stocks. Remember that you
need not select specific stocks in order to be successful with the fourteen
to nineteen week cycles. Stock index futures and OEX futures are ideal
vehicles for trading according to the fourteen to nineteen week cycles,
but these two vehicles entail considerably more risk than buying and
selling individual stocks.

Chapter 5

Short-Term Cycles in Stocks

Although there are also short-term cycles stocks and the stock averages, I do not recommend them for use by investors other than to fine tune market entry. Traditionally, short-term cycles tend to run fourteen days, twenty-eight days, and fifty-six days in length, when measured from low to low. Figures 5.1 through 5.5 are included for illustrative purposes. I do not recommend short-term cyclical applications for stock investors, but speculators should consider using short-term cycles with volatile high-priced stocks in order to capture large short-term moves. Otherwise commission costs will eat into potential profits considerably.

There are many short-term cycles. Some analysts even claim cycles of several hours in length and I'm inclined to agree with them based on my intensive research with cycles since the 1970s. If you plan to use short-term cycles for your trading then I suggest the following:

1. Research the cycles very carefully, in particular the 14- and 28-day cycles.
2. Use hourly or half-hourly stock data rather than daily. This improves your timing.
3. Avoid trading the short-term cycles in individual stocks. Rather, use one of the stock indices, preferably a broader based index such as the S&P 500 or the OEX index.
4. Always filter the cycles with timing as a confirming indicator.
5. Use very close followup stop losses to limit the size of your loss and/or the amount of drawdown in a profitable position.

FIGURE 5.1   *28–32 Day Cycles In IBM*

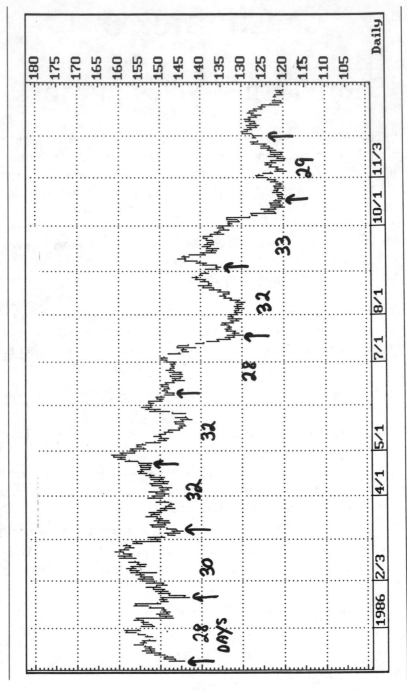

Chart reprinted with permission of Aspen Research

FIGURE 5.2 *14–19 Day Cycles in USX Corporation*

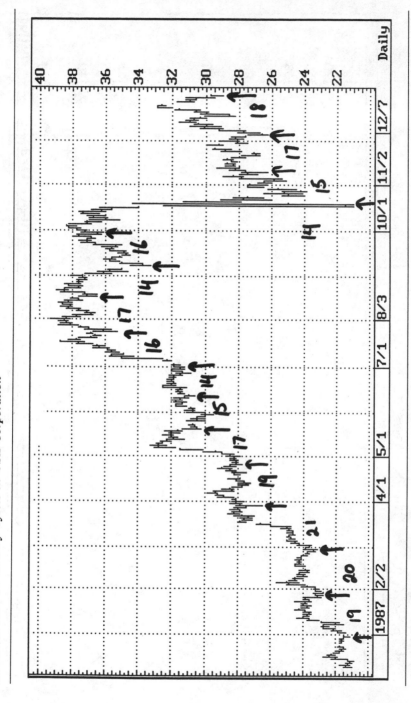

Chart reprinted with permission of Aspen Research

FIGURE 5.3 *Short-Term Cycles in Compaq Computer*

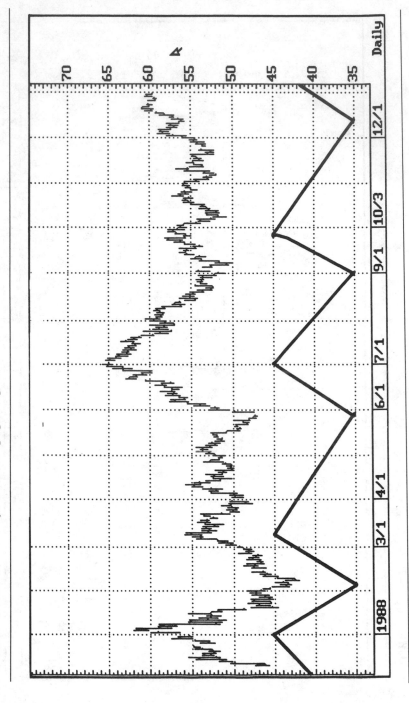

Chart reprinted with permission of Aspen Research

FIGURE 5.4 *Short-Term Cycles in Merrill Lynch*

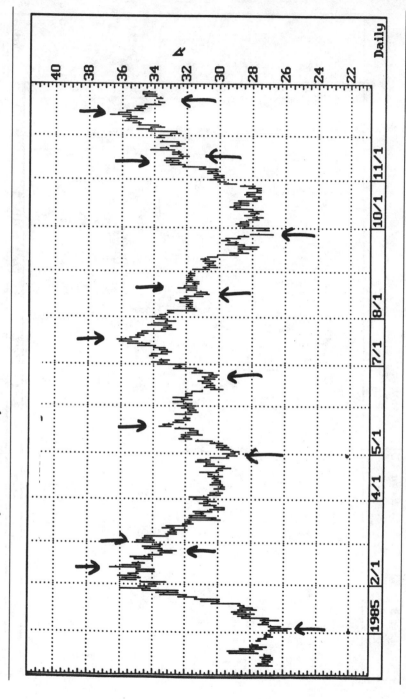

Chart reprinted with permission of Aspen Research

FIGURE 5.5 *Short-Term Cycles in USX Corporation*

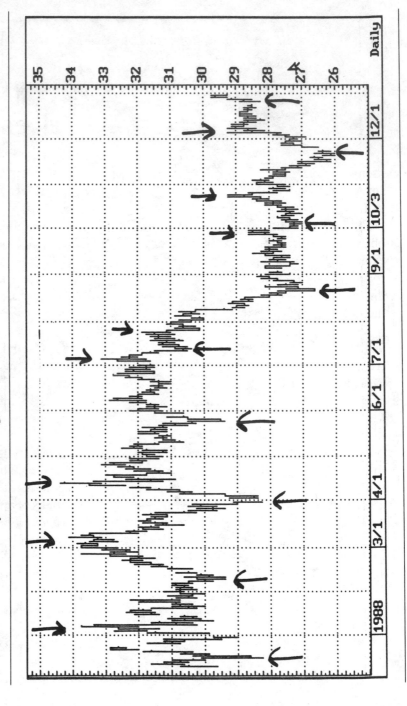

Chart reprinted with permission of Aspen Research

Chapter 6

Seasonality in Stock Prices

Seasonality refers to the tendency for the price of a given stock, stock index, commodity, or economic indicator to move in a particular direction during a given time of the year. Seasonal tendencies exist in virtually all economic data, frequently with a high degree of reliability and probability of occurrence. As an example of seasonal behavior, consider the tendency for gold prices to move higher between mid-August through late September of each year. Although this increase does not occur every year, it has been observed frequently enough to alert the astute investor or speculator to an investment or speculative opportunity. Figure 6.1 shows this tendency in gold futures prices since the late 1970s. Despite exceptions to the rule, the anticipated seasonal price increase has generally occurred. By limiting risk exposure to a predetermined dollar amount and by timing entry on the long side precisely, the speculator or investor can increase the probability of successfully following this seasonal tendency. Gold mining stocks have shown a tendency to bottom annually in August or September.

Seasonality has long been known as a significant force in agricultural commodity prices, metals, and a variety of economic data such as employment and housing starts. Yet my research has demonstrated the existence of seasonality in virtually all markets from stocks to interest rates to foreign currencies. My books *Seasonal Concepts in Futures Trading* and *Jake Bernstein's Seasonal Futures Spreads*[1] examine such tendencies and provide detailed information on reliable seasonal patterns and tendencies as well as the theory and research methodology employed in finding seasonal tendencies.

I have found that the most highly seasonal commodity and financial

---

1. Bernstein, J., *Seasonal Concepts in Futures Trading* (New York: Wiley, 1986), and *Jake Bernstein's Seasonal Futures Spreads* (New York: Wiley, 1990).

FIGURE 6.1 *Weekly Seasonal Tendency in Gold Futures*

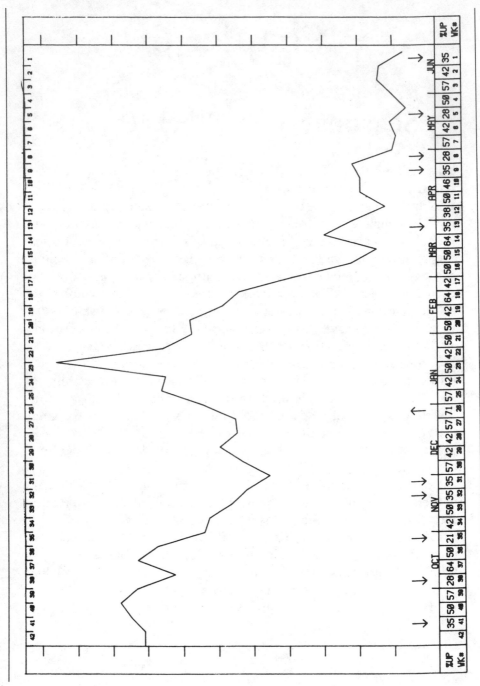

Source: MBH Commodity Advisors Inc.

markets are gold, copper, lumber, wheat, meats, foreign currencies, interest rates, and coffee. Some of these markets are so highly reliable that I actually have generated *key date trades* (KDTs) for futures traders. A KDT consists of a rule or instruction to buy or sell a given futures contract on a given date with a given stop loss in order to capitalize on a frequently observed seasonal tendency.

As an example consider the seasonal tendency in copper prices to rise during the first quarter of each year. Figure 6.2 shows this tendency in composite chart form since 1967. In other words, this chart shows average behavior of copper futures across all years. This approach allows us to isolate any seasonal tendencies that may be present in a large amount of price history. When the composite chart shows that there has been a seasonal tendency, then we can develop ways to use it to our advantage.

With seasonal price tendency charts and a highly structured computer program for researching historical data I have generated specific buy and sell dates for copper futures. An example of such a key date trade is shown in figure 6.3, along with the KDT entry and exit date data since 1967. The results are impressive. Seasonal tendencies, however, no matter how reliable they have been in the past, are not without the risk of loss. A conservative statistician would argue that more historical data would achieve a stronger comfort level with this type of data.

Now consider the seasonal tendencies in interest rates over the last 100 years or so. Figure 6.4 shows monthly cash seasonal composite charts for Treasury bill yields. If interest rates are related to stock prices, then a seasonal pattern in stocks may be worthy of investor attention and consideration. Again, we are dealing with tendencies and not with 100 percent probabilities.

Now let's turn to an examination of seasonal price behavior in stock prices. Figures 6.5 and 6.6 show monthly seasonal tendencies in the Standard & Poor's and Dow Jones industrial averages for the period of years indicated. These figures show that several months of each year exhibit seasonal behavior. Yale Hirsch in his classic *Don't Sell Stocks on Monday,* [2] a book every investor should read, concurs with this analysis.

By analyzing a vast amount of data Hirsch arrived at concise conclusions about stock prices based on repetitive patterns, a majority of

---

2. Hirsch, Y., *Don't Sell Stocks on Monday.* New York: Facts on File, 1986.

FIGURE 6.2 *Weekly Seasonal Tendency in Copper Futures*

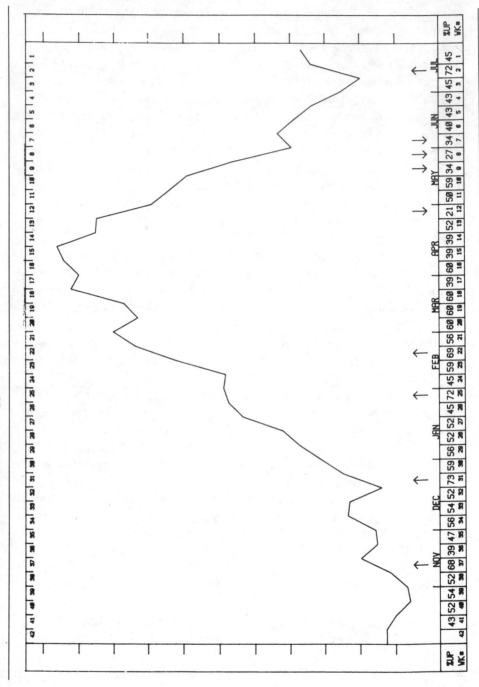

Source: MBH Commodity Advisors Inc.

FIGURE 6.3 *Copper Key Date Seasonal Trade*

Long March Copper on the close of trading 02/07
with a 6% stop loss close only, or exit on close 02/18

Entry Date:	02/07	Exit Date:	02/18
Positive Trades:	18	Negative Trades:	6
Starting Year:	1966	Ending Year:	1989
% Positive Trades:	75.00	% Negative Trades:	25.00
Average Gain:	2.95	Average Loss:	−1.49
Average Trade:	1.84	Profit/Loss Ratio:	3.000
Years Analyzed:	24	Cumulative Gain*:	$11037.50
Maximum Drawdown:	−$812.50	Calculated Stop:	0.00

Entry		Exit		Profit	Accumulated
-Date-	-Price-	-Date-	-Price-	Loss (−)	Total
02/07/66	67.20	02/18/66	71.60	4.40	4.40
02/07/67	53.10	02/20/67	50.10	−3.00	1.40
02/07/68	66.25	02/19/68	70.85	4.60	6.00
02/07/69	51.10	02/18/69	53.85	2.75	8.75
02/09/70	71.55	02/18/70	70.35	−1.20	7.55
02/08/71	45.80	02/18/71	47.50	1.70	9.25
02/07/72	49.70	02/18/72	50.70	1.00	10.25
02/07/73	54.85	02/20/73	57.20	2.35	12.60
02/07/74	93.90	02/19/74	107.10	13.20	25.80
02/07/75	52.50	02/18/75	56.40	3.90	29.70
02/09/76	55.40	02/18/76	57.30	1.90	31.60
02/07/77	66.50	02/18/77	65.00	−1.50	30.10
02/08/78	57.00	02/21/78	57.40	0.40	30.50
02/07/79	86.70	02/20/79	89.70	3.00	33.50
02/07/80	131.70	02/19/80	131.20	−0.50	33.00
02/09/81	82.70	02/18/81	80.05	−2.65	30.35
02/08/82	72.10	02/18/82	72.00	−0.10	30.25
02/07/83	73.90	02/18/83	77.85	3.95	34.20
02/07/84	63.45	02/21/84	64.75	1.30	35.50
02/07/85	61.40	02/19/85	61.85	0.45	35.95
02/07/86	63.90	02/18/86	64.25	0.35	36.30
02/09/87	61.10	02/18/87	63.00	1.90	38.20
02/08/88	95.80	02/18/88	98.75	2.95	41.15
02/07/89	131.50	02/21/89	134.50	3.00	44.15

Source: MBH Commodity Advisors Inc.

FIGURE 6.4 *Monthly Seasonal Cash Tendency T Bill Yields*

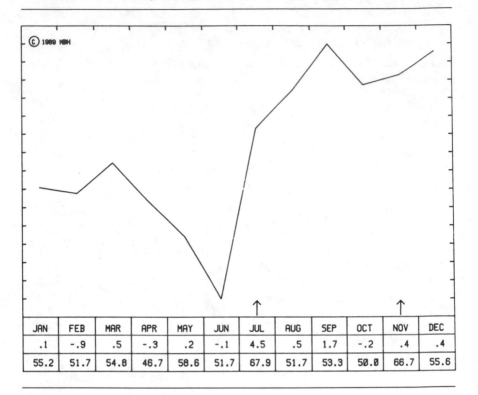

JAN	FEB	MAR	APR	MAY	JUN	JUL	AUG	SEP	OCT	NOV	DEC
.1	-.9	.5	-.3	.2	-.1	4.5	.5	1.7	-.2	.4	.4
55.2	51.7	54.8	46.7	58.6	51.7	67.9	51.7	53.3	50.0	66.7	55.6

Source: MBH Commodity Advisors Inc.

which are either seasonal or variations on the seasonal theme. His work with the well-known January barometer and his monthly seasonal analyses are shown in figures 6.7 and 6.8.

It's hard to argue with seasonal price tendencies. Whether you're a fundamental-oriented investor, a long-term investor, or a short-term speculator, you should have a working knowledge of seasonal price tendencies to improve your timing.

Let's look at my weekly S&P composite seasonal tendency chart (figure 6.9). This chart combines weekly cash S&P from 1936 through 1982 with weekly December S&P futures from 1982 through 1988. The numbers along the bottom row show the approximate week number for the year and the row above it (marked "% Up") the percentage of time

FIGURE 6.5 *Monthly Seasonal Tendency in Cash S&P*

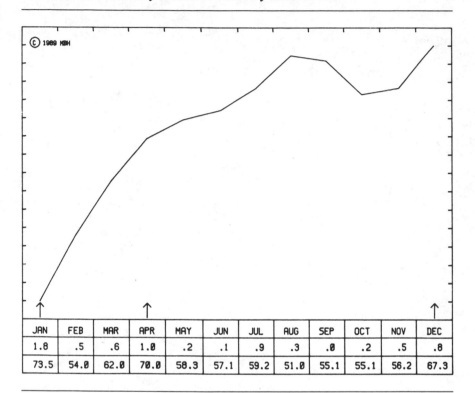

JAN	FEB	MAR	APR	MAY	JUN	JUL	AUG	SEP	OCT	NOV	DEC
1.8	.5	.6	1.0	.2	.1	.9	.3	.0	.2	.5	.8
73.5	54.0	62.0	70.0	58.3	57.1	59.2	51.0	55.1	55.1	56.2	67.3

Source: MBH Commodity Advisors Inc.

that the price has ended the week higher than the previous week. Because the figures show percentage of time up, those below 50 must be subtracted from 100 to arrive at the percentage of time down for the week. For example, consider week seven, which reads 40 percent. This means that prices have gone down 60 percent of the time for this week. The chart shows arrows for weeks that have a high percentage of time tendency. All of the arrows are up, suggesting that since 1936 there have been no highly reliable down weeks, and, in fact, since 1936 stocks have been in a secular bull market. Should the secular trend change, then the readings over time are likely to show reliable down weeks.

In bull markets the weeks shown are likely to be particularly strong and reliable to the up side, while in bear markets I suggest you watch

FIGURE 6.6   *Monthly Seasonal Tendency in Stocks, 1790–1989*

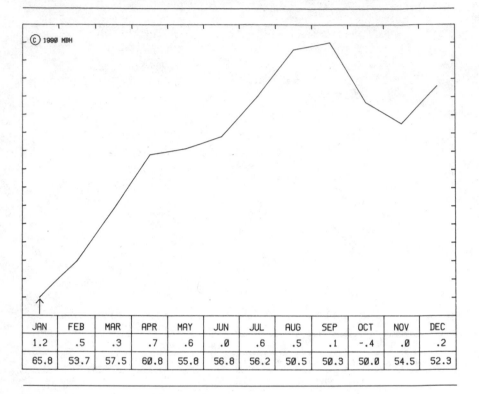

JAN	FEB	MAR	APR	MAY	JUN	JUL	AUG	SEP	OCT	NOV	DEC
1.2	.5	.3	.7	.6	.0	.6	.5	.1	-.4	.0	.2
65.8	53.7	57.5	60.8	55.8	56.8	56.2	50.5	50.3	50.0	54.5	52.3

Source: MBH Commodity Advisors Inc.

closely weeks thirty-three, twenty-three, and seven. Remember that each year contains a different number of Fridays. This chart was constructed on a last-trading-day-of-the-week to last-trading-day-of-the-week basis, so you must shift the calendar somewhat to adjust it to the current year.

Another approach to seasonality is what I have termed *array analysis*. In this technique a large amount of data is fitted into a statistical array so that one month (or week if we construct a weekly array analysis) can be compared with all months in order to determine how often prices have been higher or lower on a comparative basis. Array analysis provides answers to questions such as "How often have monthly average stock prices been higher in November than they have

FIGURE 6.7 *The January Barometer in Stocks*

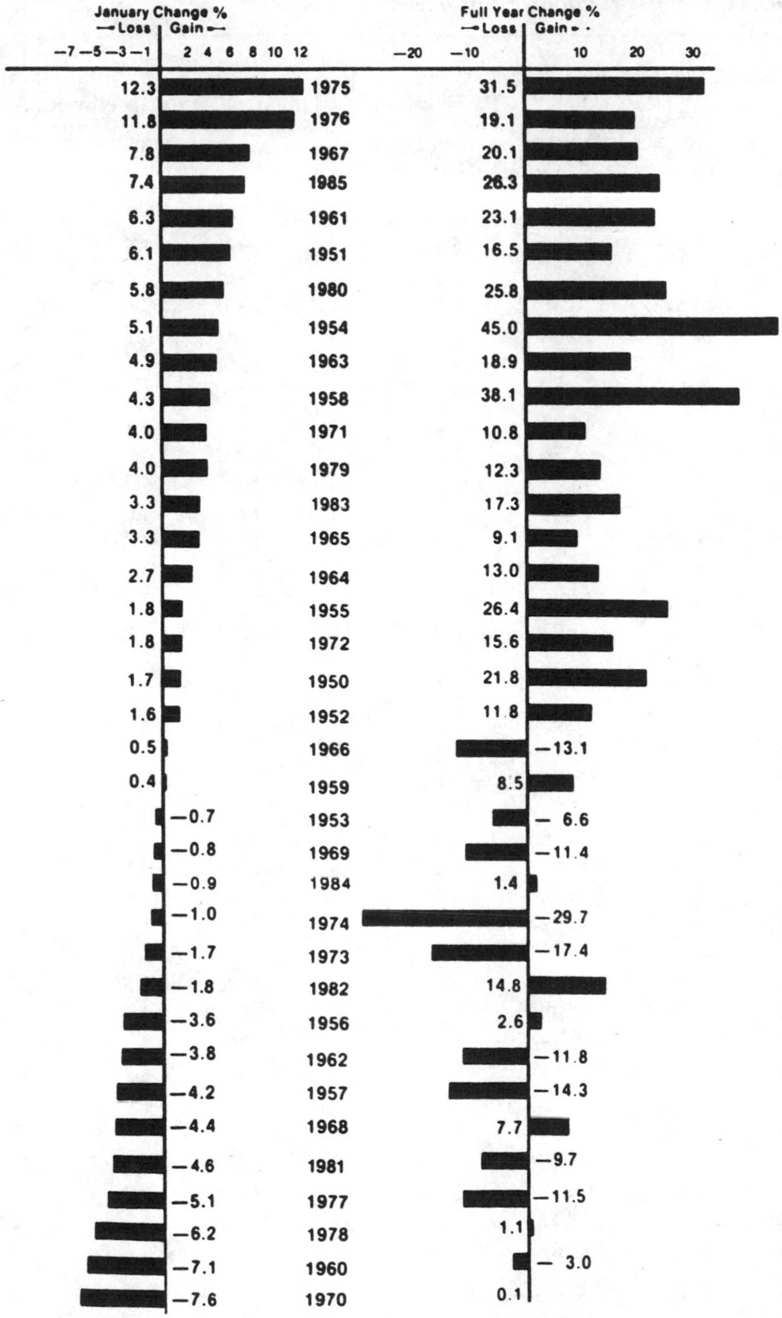

January Change %
Loss | Gain
−7 −5 −3 −1 2 4 6 8 10 12
Full Year Change %
Loss | Gain
−20 −10 10 20 30
12.3 1975 31.5
11.8 1976 19.1
7.8 1967 20.1
7.4 1985 26.3
6.3 1961 23.1
6.1 1951 16.5
5.8 1980 25.8
5.1 1954 45.0
4.9 1963 18.9
4.3 1958 38.1
4.0 1971 10.8
4.0 1979 12.3
3.3 1983 17.3
3.3 1965 9.1
2.7 1964 13.0
1.8 1955 26.4
1.8 1972 15.6
1.7 1950 21.8
1.6 1952 11.8
0.5 1966 −13.1
0.4 1959 8.5
−0.7 1953 − 6.6
−0.8 1969 −11.4
−0.9 1984 1.4
−1.0 1974 −29.7
−1.7 1973 −17.4
−1.8 1982 14.8
−3.6 1956 2.6
−3.8 1962 −11.8
−4.2 1957 −14.3
−4.4 1968 7.7
−4.6 1981 −9.7
−5.1 1977 −11.5
−6.2 1978 1.1
−7.1 1960 − 3.0
−7.6 1970 0.1

Source: Hirsch, Yale. *Don't Sell Stocks on Monday.* New York: Facts on File, 1986.

FIGURE 6.8   *The January Barometer in Stocks*

Year	Market Performance in January Previous Year's Close	January Close	January Change	Rank	Year	January Change	Year's Change
				|←— January Performance by Rank —→|			
1950	16.76[a]	17.05[a]	1.7%	1.	1975	12.3%	31.5%
1951	20.41	21.66	6.1	2.	1976	11.8	19.1
1952	23.77	24.14	1.6	3.	1967	7.8	20.1
1953	26.57	26.38	−0.7	4.	1985	7.4	26.3
1954	24.81	26.08	5.1	5.	1961	6.3	23.1
1955	35.98	36.63	1.8	6.	1951	6.1	16.5
1956	45.48	43.82	−3.7	7.	1980	5.8	25.8
1957	46.67	44.72	−4.2	8.	1954	5.1	45.0
1958	39.99	41.70	4.3	9.	1963	4.9	18.9
1959	55.21	55.42	0.4	10.	1958	4.3	38.1
1960	59.89	55.61	−7.1	11.	1971	4.0	10.8
1961	58.11	61.78	6.3	12.	1979	4.0	12.3
1962	71.55	68.84	−3.8	13.	1983	3.3	17.3
1963	63.10	66.20	4.9	14.	1965	3.3	9.1
1964	75.02	77.04	2.7	15.	1964	2.7	13.0
1965	84.75	87.56	3.3	16.	1955	1.8	26.4
1966	92.43	92.88	0.5	17.	1972	1.8	15.6
1967	80.33	86.61	7.8	18.	1950	1.7	21.8
1968	96.47	92.24	−4.4	19.	1952	1.6	11.8
1969	103.86	103.01	−0.8	20.	1966	0.5	−13.1
1970	92.06	85.02	−7.6	21.	1959	0.4	8.5
1971	92.15	95.88	4.0	22.	1953	−0.7	−6.6
1972	102.09	103.94	1.8	23.	1969	−0.8	−11.4
1973	118.05	116.03	−1.7	24.	1984	−0.9	1.4
1974	97.55	96.57	−1.0	25.	1974	−1.0	−29.7
1975	68.56	76.98	12.3	26.	1973	−1.7	−17.4
1976	90.19	100.86	11.8	27.	1982	−1.8	14.8
1977	107.46	102.03	−5.1	28.	1956	−3.6	2.6
1978	95.10	89.25	−6.2	29.	1962	−3.8	−11.8
1979	96.11	99.93	4.0	30.	1957	−4.2	−14.3
1980	107.94	114.16	5.8	31.	1968	−4.4	7.7
1981	135.76	129.55	−4.6	32.	1981	−4.6	−9.7
1982	122.55	120.40	−1.8	33.	1977	−5.1	−11.5
1983	140.64	145.30	3.3	34.	1978	−6.2	1.1
1984	164.93	163.41	−0.9	35.	1960	−7.1	−3.0
1985	167.24	179.63	7.4	36.	1970	−7.6	0.1

Source: Hirsch, Yale. *Don't Sell Stocks on Monday.* New York: Facts on File, 1986.

FIGURE 6.9 *Composite Weekly Seasonal S&P Chart*

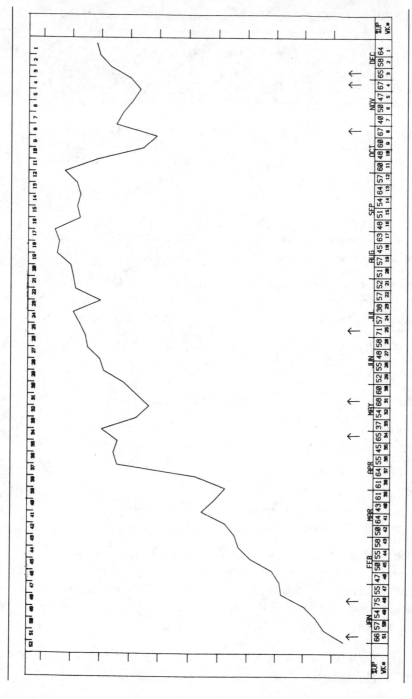

Source: MBH Commodity Advisors Inc.

FIGURE 6.10   *S&P Monthly Array Analysis 1959–1989*

	Jan	Feb	Mar	Apr	May	Jun	Jul	Aug	Sep	Oct	Nov	Dec
Jan		54.8	[64.5]	[64.5]	61.3	58.1	58.1	61.3	[64.5]	[64.5]	58.1	[64.5]
Feb			61.3	[64.5]	[64.5]	61.3	[64.5]	[67.7]	[67.7]	[64.5]	61.3	[71.0]
Mar				[74.2]	61.3	61.3	54.8	61.3	[64.5]	61.3	[64.5]	[67.7]
Apr					53.3	−51.6	54.8	61.3	58.1	54.8	58.1	[67.7]
May						50.0	−56.7	60.0	53.3	60.0	60.0	60.0
Jun							−53.3	56.7	60.0	58.6	50.0	60.0
Jul								53.3	56.7	53.3	53.3	[63.3]
Aug									53.3	53.3	60.0	[70.0]
Sep										53.3	[63.3]	[63.3]
Oct											62.1	[70.0]
Nov												[66.7]

Source: MBH Commodity Advisors Inc.

FIGURE 6.11   *Seasonal Array Analysis S&P 1940–1989*

	Jan	Feb	Mar	Apr	May	Jun	Jul	Aug	Sep	Oct	Nov	Dec
Jan		54.0	58.0	62.0	62.0	62.0	[64.0]	[64.0]	[64.0]	[68.0]	[64.0]	[66.0]
Feb			62.0	[66.0]	[64.0]	62.0	[64.0]	[70.0]	[72.0]	[66.0]	[64.0]	[70.0]
Mar				[70.0]	59.2	62.0	[66.0]	[72.0]	[66.0]	[64.0]	[66.0]	[66.0]
Apr					57.1	56.0	62.0	[70.0]	[64.0]	62.0	58.0	[68.0]
May						57.1	52.1	61.2	[63.3]	[65.3]	61.2	59.2
Jun							59.2	61.2	[63.3]	62.5	57.1	[65.3]
Jul								51.0	53.1	−51.0	53.1	[63.3]
Aug									55.1	55.1	57.1	[67.3]
Sep										55.1	[63.3]	61.2
Oct											56.2	[67.3]
Nov												[67.3]

Source: MBH Commodity Advisors Inc.

been in March?" or "How often have monthly average stock prices been lower in April than they have been in January?" Figure 6.10 shows an array analysis for S&P from 1959 through 1989 and figure 6.11 shows an array analysis from 1940 through 1989. Here are a few of the insights I've gained through my research:

1. Stock prices show a marked tendency to rise during January.
2. The first week of the new year usually has been bullish.

3. Although February and March have been bullish months, they have not been predictably bullish, but when prices have moved higher in February and March, the size of the moves has been relatively large.

4. A corrective decline is likely from mid-March through early April.

5. April often has been a high volatility month.

6. The last week of April has shown a high rally probability.

7. The first two weeks of April have shown a tendency to the up side.

8. April up moves have shown a tendency to be rather large.

9. If you're looking for explanations, the April findings are confirmed and explained by Yale Hirsch (shown in figure 6.12).

10. An early May decline usually follows the April rally.

11. An existing uptrend tends to slow from May through August.

FIGURE 6.12 *Yale Hirsch's Explanation of the April Seasonal Stock Rally*

Numero Uno . . . April

The hottest month in recent years has been April, with 464.06 Dow points gained since 1950. Over 120 of these points were netted in 1982 and 1983, probably due to the newly enacted legislation making IRA accounts more attractive. This may have triggered a massive inflow of funds.

Here's why: Few people realize that the forty million existing IRA accounts must now have their contributions deposited by April 15. This means that some $30 to $40 billion hit the banks and the mutual funds, with a chunk of it surely winding up in the stock market.

Consider also that of the billions already in IRAs any year end, a good portion are in maturing certificates of deposit which need to be rolled over. If interest rates are low or falling and stocks are buoyant, you can bet some of that money will find its way to Wall Street. If you add the billions in money market funds at a time of shrinking interest rates, the possibilities for the market become mind-boggling. And if the decision to invest is held up temporarily, pressures can build up which can rocket the Dow as it did in August 1984 up 109 points or in May and June 1985 up 77 points.

Source: Hirsch, Yale: *Don't Sell Stocks on Monday.* New York: Facts on File, 1986.

12. The summer rally is not as reliable an event as some would have us believe, but the first week of July does show a good probability of higher prices.

13. August has been a time for tops.

14. September tends to be a down month.

15. Seasonal lows and possibly large declines tend to occur in October, usually by midmonth (consider the October stock crashes).

16. A year-end rally is common and is particularly likely to begin in late October and last through early November.

As you can see, stock prices have displayed a marked seasonal tendency. I am also convinced of the seasonal tendencies of individual stocks and stock groups. As computer technology becomes increasingly available to handle large relational data bases, we will be able to extract even more meaningful data about broad stock behavior and individual stocks as well.

Chapter 7

Risk Management

Perhaps the single most important ingredient for success in stock trading is risk management. Although an investor may be adept at stock selection and timing, the ability to effectively manage risk is even more important than good timing. In a rising market most stocks will rise, and in a falling market most stocks will fall. Legendary stock trader Jesse Livermore was quick to point out the fact that unless the market trend is in your favor, your odds of making money are not good. The following comments are from *Reminiscences of a Stock Market Operator,* written under Livermore's pseudonym Edwin LeFevbre:

> I never hesitate to tell a man that I am bullish or bearish. But I do not tell people to buy or sell any particular stock. In a bear market all stocks go down and in a bull market they go up. . . . I have often said that to buy on a rising market is the most comfortable way of buying stocks . . .[1]

But Livermore was not alone in asserting that traders must make their moves consistent with the direction of the major trend. In a rising market you are unlikely to lose money by buying stocks, provided that you do not buy near the end of the existing trend. Conversely, in a falling market you are unlikely to lose money if you sell stocks short unless you sell near the end of the trend. The individual who makes investment decisions consistent with the cycles described in this book greatly increases his or her odds of making money. When stocks are in a bullish trend, the temptation to ride losses on the long side is considerably greater than when stocks are in a falling trend. The investor may

1. LeFevbre, Edwin, *Reminiscences of a Stock Market Operator* (Larchmont, NY: American Research Council, 1965).

cling to long positions in the expectation that the rising general market trend will eventually bail out the losing position. Occasionally, however, this does not happen, and the investor finds that the losing position keeps getting worse. Eventually the bull market is over, but the losing investment is still being held as the overall market trend turns lower and the losing stock or stocks continue their deteriorating trend. In fact, since markets tend to fall faster than they rise, the losing trend is often exacerbated and the losses continue to mount. The investor may hold the losing position until many of the profits realized on other investments have been eaten up by the one investment that went sour and should have been liquidated many months or perhaps several years earlier.

Many investors and speculators are guilty of such poor decisions in risk management. I quote again from *Reminiscences of a Stock Market Operator* (LeFevbre, E. 1965: 119): "A loss never bothers me after I take it. I forget it overnight. But being wrong—not taking the loss—that is what does damage to the pocketbook and to the soul."

Your own experiences and what you have read in this chapter demonstrate that inappropriately dealing with losses often proves to be the most significant cause for failure in investing. Worse yet, one error often leads to other errors. By riding a loss you tie up capital, and by tying up capital you miss good opportunities that may come your way. There are several ways to minimize or entirely avoid this error.

Develop a Specific Plan and Implement It

By developing a specific investment plan and by adhering as closely as possible to your plan you automatically avoid serious errors such as riding a loss beyond your predetermined risk point. Here are some suggestions for implementing such a plan:

1. Determine the major cyclical trend.
2. Study industry group cycles.
3. Select stocks that you feel confident will move in the direction of the anticipated market trend.

4. Watch for timing indicators to confirm the current trend.

5. If a trend has started recently or if the market is still in the early stages of a cyclical move, then take the appropriate action in the stocks you have selected.

6. Determine in advance how much of a loss you are willing to accept for each stock you have selected. This determination can be made on the basis of technical indicators or by a strict dollar or percentage loss. For example, assume you buy IBM based on a combination of a cyclical low and a buy signal on timing indicators. You can exit once a sell signal has developed; you can sell if the stock makes a new intraday low for this particular move or wave; you can sell if the stock makes a new closing price low for this move; you can decide ahead of time that you will take your loss if the stock goes against you by a given percentage of the price you paid for it. In any case, you must determine ahead of time what your risk limitation rule will be and then implement your decision strictly.

7. Whatever risk management method you choose, attempt to lock in the risk by giving your broker a precise stop loss, preferably in the form of a "good until cancelled" order. In so doing you will be less likely to alter your stop loss point. Hence, you will be placing a strict limit on the dollar amount of loss you will accept on each position. By limiting losses, and by allowing profitable positions to run, you will be practicing the most important rules of effective money management.

8. A more advanced tack you can take is to use stock options to limit your risk once you are in a profitable position. Assume, for example, that you purchased GM at or near a cyclical bottom and after confirmation by timing signals. Assume also that the stock has moved $20 in your favor. You could protect your profit by buying put options as insurance against a possibly sizeable decline. What you stand to make on the put increasing in value as the stock declines could very well protect you from the stock's decline. If the trend continues higher, however, then the put will expire worthless, and you will have forfeited the put premium value plus commission as the cost of your insurance policy.

Other stock option strategies can be employed to protect your long or short position in a stock or to maximize your overall rate of return on your investments, but they are beyond the scope of this book. Numerous excellent books have been written about this particular approach.

9. It is always a good idea to obtain assistance in implementing your plan, particularly if you tend to change your plan when the time comes to accept a loss. I recommend recruiting an investing partner or partners who will help oversee the discipline in your program. Forming an investment club can be a good solution. Decisions made by groups, although often considerably more difficult to achieve, also tend to be more effective decisions and are more likely to be implemented exactly according to specifications than decisions made and carried out by a single individual.

10. You also can attempt to get help from your broker. A word of caution is in order if you decide to do so. Brokers earn money by generating commission dollars. This motivation may be conscious or unconscious, but beware of allowing your decisions to be swayed by the influence of your broker. I am not calling into question the ethics of brokers but merely pointing out a problem that goes with the territory of being a broker. Most brokers are ethical and interested in what is best for their clients. Discount brokers who do not dispense advice do not present a conflict-of-interest problem, but you may find it difficult to obtain from them information you require to reach a decision about stock selections.

Avoid Tips, Rumors, and Impulsive Decisions

On occasion you may find it profitable to act on tips or rumors, but in most cases such a break in discipline does not prove profitable and may, in fact, divert your funds from a more logical and promising course of action.

Here are some suggestions on how to avoid tip taking and rumor following.

1. Inform your friends, relatives, business associates, and brokers, that you do not want to be bothered by tips and rumors.

2. Work with a partner, associate, or investment club in order to reduce the possibility that you will act on impulse.

3. If you have found a good stock market advisory service or newsletter, then follow its recommendations precisely, or better yet, have a broker follow it for you. This eliminates you from the equation and reduces the probability of impulsive actions.

4. Instead of buying or selling individual stocks use some of the switch mutual funds as your investment vehicles. This reduces the probability that you will act on tips or rumors in individual stocks.

5. Avoid reading publications that may prompt you to actions not in keeping with your investment plan. There is nothing wrong with reading the financial press, but you may find that you are unable to remain true to your plan after reading what the so-called experts have to say. You also may find yourself wanting to act on stocks or industry groups that have received media attention. If you aren't strong enough to rationally evaluate the opinions of others, no matter how respected they may be, then avoid reading all financial publications.

6. Some people are prompted to action by watching television. Since the early 1980s cable television has brought most Americans closer to the ongoing financial news than ever before. Financial News Network, (FNN) for example, has a long broadcasting day that begins early in the morning with news of overseas markets and ends late each day with statistical overviews of the day's activity. Throughout the day FNN features interviews with market analysts, brokers, investment advisors, and others in virtually every area of investments from stocks to futures and from precious metals to bonds. I have been a featured expert on numerous occasions and have appeared regularly as a guest commentator, and I have seen firsthand how the opinions of experts can sway investors to action, particularly when such opinions are strong, well researched, articulately expressed, and seemingly logical. These financial news programs educate investors and inform them of new opportunities. Yet some individuals cannot avoid being inappropriately influenced by such information.

The information you obtain must be used logically and unemotionally before it can benefit your investment program. Specific investment needs and objectives are unique to the individual: a single middle-aged male invests differently than an elderly widower does. You must not act on the basis of what sounds right or on the basis of a perceived rate of return but only on information that is consistent with your program. Hence, I suggest you approach financially oriented tips and rumors logically, conservatively, and with healthy skepticism. Don't be afraid to ask questions. If you have an opportunity to call in to a television or radio show, then do so. Question the statistics, logic, and claims you are hearing. If you still like what you hear, take the time to think it through, do your own research, and ask more questions. It is only after such diligence that you should take appropriate action.

Consider a Money Manager or Mutual Fund

Many money managers and mutual funds have achieved excellent and consistent performance records in stocks. I recommend that a portion of your available capital be placed with such individuals or firms. Successful money managers are known for their discipline and consistency. If you have a given portion of your available investment capital well placed with several such funds or managers, then you will be relatively certain to benefit in strong markets. You can even participate in more aggressively managed programs that show gains or relatively small losses in declining markets due to their ability to take large cash positions early or in advance of downturns or to use stock index futures to hedge their portfolios against declines.

Diversify

Much can be said in favor of diversification. Diversification is essential to a well-rounded portfolio, yet it is also an individual matter. A diversified portfolio for one type of investor will be totally different from a diversified portfolio that is appropriate for another type of investor. The basic considerations are financial ability, age, tax situation, and goals.

A financial planner or accountant who is familiar with your needs should be consulted to determine the mix of investments you should have in your portfolio. I suggest you read several of the many books on this subject. I also suggest you plan your investment portfolio before you invest a single dollar.

Make Time for Your Market Work

One of the most serious errors an investor can commit is to be inconsistent about market studies. Successful investing is not a hobby; it's a job. And because it is a job, it requires time, effort, and consistency. Set aside specific hours for your market studies. How much time is a function of how much work you have and how much money you are investing. Make a schedule and stick to it. Active investors or stock traders may need to spend several hours each day doing their homework, while those with small portfolios or long-term goals may need to spend only several hours a week on their work. I also recommend that you work while the markets are closed to avoid being unduly influenced by current market behavior and events that might affect short-term market trends.

Chapter 8

Basic Cyclical Timing and Stocks

This book has stressed the importance of timing in conjunction with cyclical tendencies in the stock market. The following steps summarize how investors should use cyclical patterns with stocks:

1. Determine the current cyclical trend and when the trend last changed.
2. Determine whether the stock market averages have turned and whether timing indicators confirm the market turn or change in cycle.
3. Select the stocks in which you wish to invest.
4. Confirm your selections by applying timing indicators to each.
5. Take the prescribed action (i.e. buy or sell) using an appropriate risk management or stop loss program.

A significant part of this process involves the application of timing indicators. Although timing in some markets is not critical, it is very important in others, such as in futures trading, where margins are from 1 to 3 percent of the total contract value. Market entry even thirty minutes too early or too late can mean the difference between profit and loss in the futures market. In real estate, on the other hand, timing is not as critical. An investor may make a timing error, but often there is time to extricate oneself from the error without a major loss. Timing decisions are determined by two variables: time and margin. The shorter the investor's time frame and the lower the margin, the more critical the timing—and the more critical the timing, the more sophisticated the timing tools must be. Although the futures trader may require complicated programs and indicators in order to compensate for low margins and short time frames, the stock investor need not be as concerned with complex timing indicators. Traditional timing methods usually are more than sufficient for the stock investor to confirm cyclical market turns and concise times to enter stocks. Among these indicators are the following:

1. Traditional chart patterns such as pennants, triangles, saucer bottoms, head-and-shoulders formations, island tops and bottoms, and gaps;
2. Trend-line support and resistance analysis and trend-line breakouts;
3. Price bar formations;
4. Moving averages and variations on the moving-average theme.

Most traditional chart patterns are open to interpretation, but I have found trend-line breakouts, moving averages, and price bar signals to be more objective. Specific indicators are not ordinarily subject to interpretation and therefore can be applied objectively. Some analysts prefer to use various wave patterns (such as the Elliott wave and Gann angle), but such patterns also are subject to interpretation and difficult for many investors to understand. Through the years I also have been concerned about the disagreement I've seen among analysts who use the same tools to make their forecasts and stock selections. Although the methods described in this book are not totally objective, they are well over 90 percent objective, and there is little room for subjectivity or interpretation when they are used in conjunction with cycles. I feel that market tools such as Gann angles and Elliott waves are intended for use by professional market analysts and not by average investors. This book intends to provide the average investor with specific tools that are both simple to understand and equally simple to calculate and apply.

Simple Trend-Line Analysis

A *trend line* is a straight line connecting three or more price points on a chart. Two major types of trend lines are used in traditional chart analysis: *support lines,* which are drawn in an upward direction under price lows, and *resistance lines,* which are drawn in a downward direction above price highs. Schematically we can represent support and resistance trend lines as shown in Figures 8.1 and 8.2.

Stock prices move in trends, and drawing support lines under upward trends and resistance lines above downward trends helps investors determine when prices have changed their direction. Figures 8.3 and 8.4 show various support and resistance trend-line breakouts and buy (B)/sell (S) signals resulting from trendline penetrations.

Trend-line analysis is known to virtually all technical traders and is widely used. As effective as it appears to be, however, there are some definite limitations to trend-line application as a sole method of timing stock transactions. The first and most significant of these limitations is that there are no strictly operational or mechanical rules for the use of trend lines. We assume that a stock should be bought when it breaks out above a resistance trend line and sold when it breaks out below a support line, but these rules represent ideal conditions. Stocks frequently penetrate their trend lines only to resume their previous trend. Such false signals tend to lead to losses and to liquidation of positions prior to the end of a move. Once a position has been closed out, it is often difficult to time appropriate reentry. Books on technical stock analysis usually include case scenarios that are misleading. Although the textbook cases will help you make money, there are more situations that fail to conform to expectations than there are situations that follow the rules perfectly.

Another limitation of trend-line analysis is that there are no definitive rules for drawing the lines. How close must a price come to the trend line to be considered a touch of the line? How much of a penetration is considered a true penetration of the line? How thick should the line be? How long should a trend line be? These questions relate to the art of trend-line application as opposed to the science of trend-line analysis, and pure trend-line analysis is more of an art than a science. Most good trend-line analysts use more of their intuitive talents than their learned skills.

How can trend-line applications be salvaged? Are they worth using? I maintain that trend-line analysis can be a powerful tool under the following conditions:

1. Trend lines should connect at least three points, preferably more.
2. Trend lines can be more effective when closing price line charts are analyzed as opposed to high/low bar charts. Figure 8.5 shows the same market using a high/low/close price bar chart and a

FIGURE 8.1 *Support and Resistance Trend Lines, General Electric (GE)*

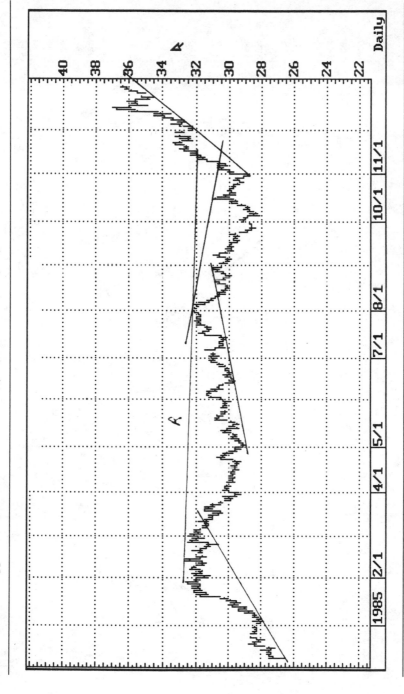

Chart courtesy of Aspen Research

FIGURE 8.2 *Support and Resistance Trend Lines, Teledyne Inc. (TDY)*

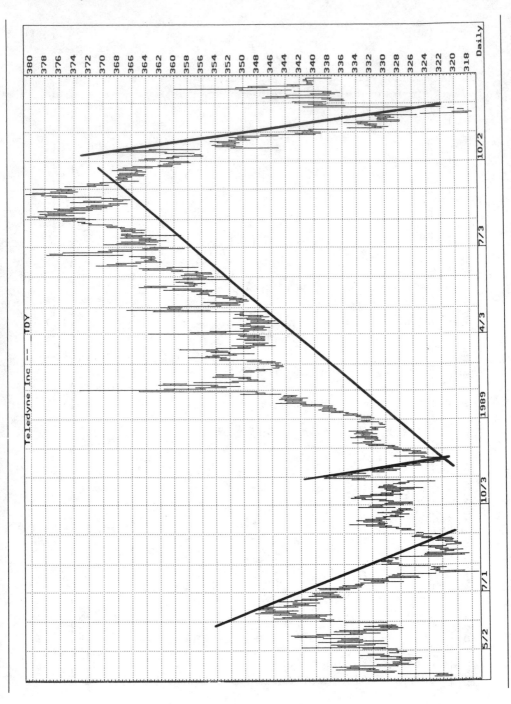

Chart courtesy of Aspen Research

FIGURE 8.3 *Trend-Line Support and Resistance Breakout, Chrysler Corp. (C)*

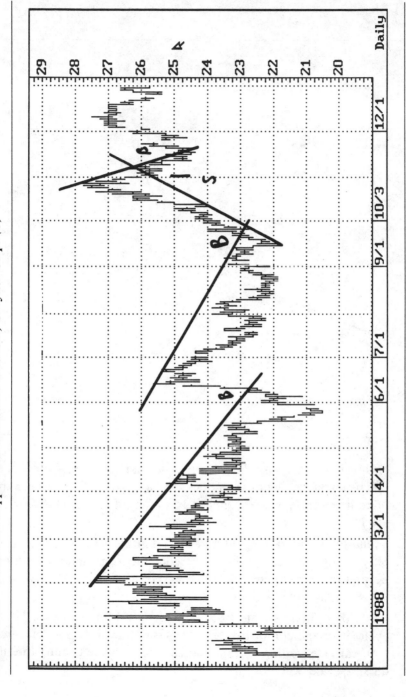

Chart courtesy of Aspen Research

FIGURE 8.4   *Trend-Line Support and Resistance Breakout, General Electric (GE)*

Chart courtesy of Aspen Research

closing line chart only. The closing line chart gives different trend-line penetration signals than does the bar chart. I feel that closing price line charts are less subject to errors of interpretation than are bar charts.

3. Trend-line penetrations should be definitive. Hesitate to accept only a single penetration of the trend line as a signal for action. Several successive penetrations should be used for generating market entry and exit signals.

4. Additional filters should be used with trend-line analysis. Using cycles in conjunction with trend lines is not the only possible filter. You can use trading volume indicators, advance-decline line indicators, and so on.

FIGURE 8.5 *Comparison of Bar Chart and Closing Price Chart*

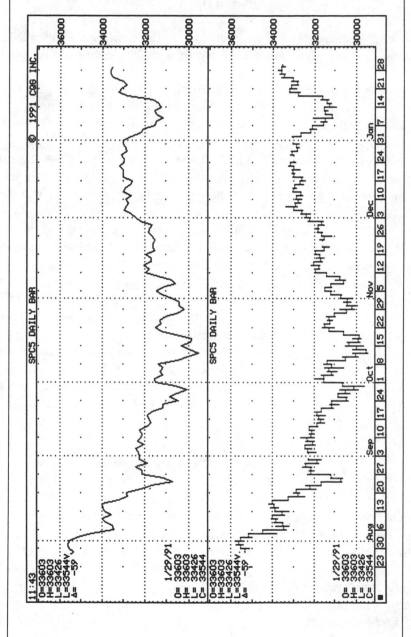

Chart Courtesy of Commodity Quote Graphics

How to Use Support and Resistance Lines with Cycles

Support lines can be used as levels for buying stocks once the cycle has turned bullish. Resistance lines can be used for selling stocks once a cycle has turned bearish. Assume that you are like many investors; you know that the market has turned bullish but you are afraid to buy. Assume also that the market had turned bullish over six months ago and you realize that you have missed the boat. You are still afraid to follow the strength in stocks for fear that you may be buying close to the top of a move. What to do? Find a stock that has been participating in the bull market. Draw a support line under prices. Wait until prices pull back to support. Buy at support. A good way to avoid watching the stocks you wish to buy on a pullback to support is to place a good-until-cancelled (GTC) order with your broker. If and when stock prices react to the down side, you will likely be filled as prices enter the strong support area suggested by the support line.

Resistance lines can be used in several ways as well. Assume that you are long stocks when a cyclical top forms and that you want to take action once a trend to the down side has clearly formed. In other words, you want to sell your stocks but not prematurely. You want definitive evidence that a top has come. What to do? Wait until you are certain that the major stock cycle has turned lower. Wait for your stocks to approach trend-line resistance, and then sell them. If you are an aggressive trader, you can take a short position using trend-line analysis. You could also sell or buy on trend-line breakouts.

Using Trend-Line Breakouts with Cycles

Another way to use trend lines is to watch for breakouts. A breakout occurs when prices close above a resistance line or below a support line, but only as they are consistent with the cycles. A cyclical bottom is a signal to buy on breakouts above resistance lines, and a cyclical top, to sell on breakouts below support lines. Figures 8.6 and 8.7 illustrate this situation for each of these two conditions, and figures 8.8 through 8.10 show some additional examples of this application.

Trend-line breakouts can be used with individual stocks, various

FIGURE 8.6 *Ideal Combination of Cycle Tops and Support Line Sell Signals, Walt Disney Co.*

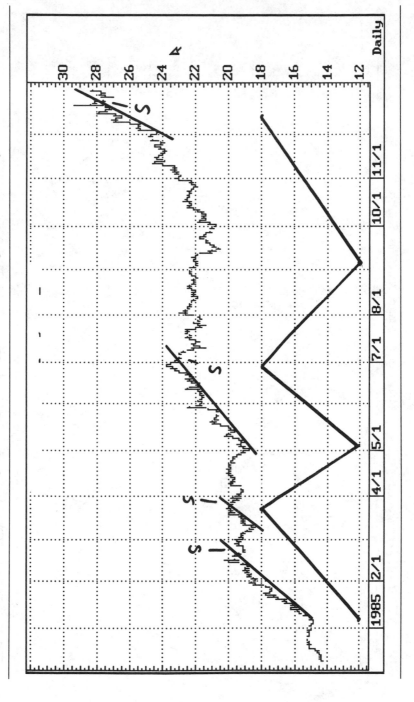

FIGURE 8.7   Ideal Combination of Cycle Bottoms and Resistance Line Buy Signals

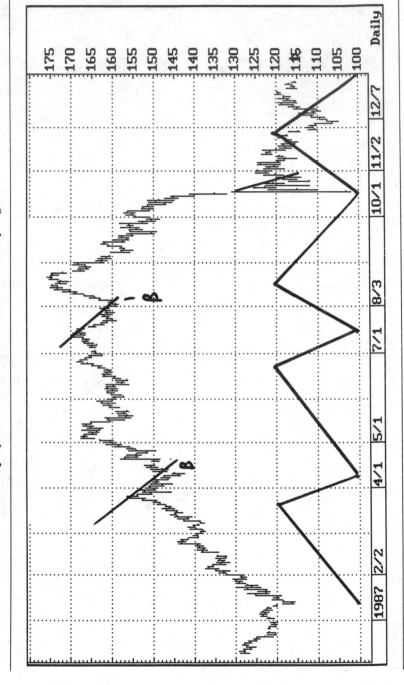

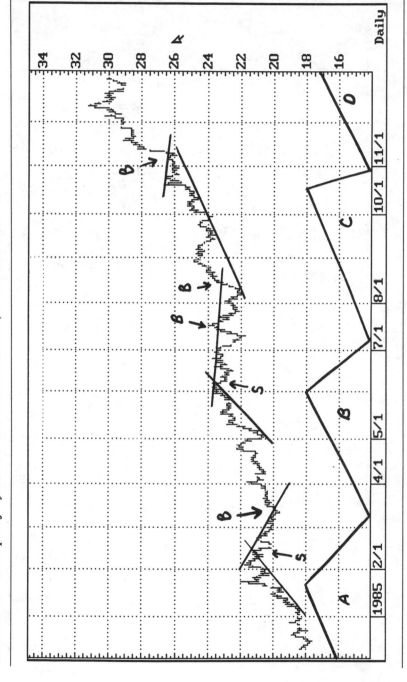

FIGURE 8.8 *Example of Cycles and Trend Line Breakouts, F. W. Woolworth Co.*

FIGURE 8.9   *Example of Cycles and Trend Line Breakouts, General Electric (GE)*

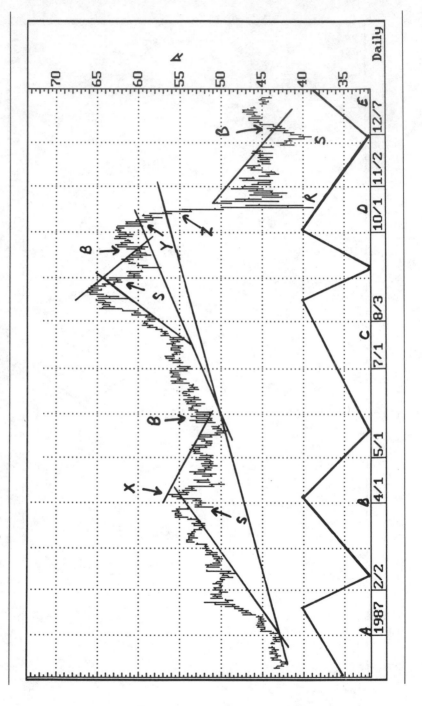

FIGURE 8.10 *Example of Cycles and Trend Line Breakouts, Teledyne Inc. (TDY)*

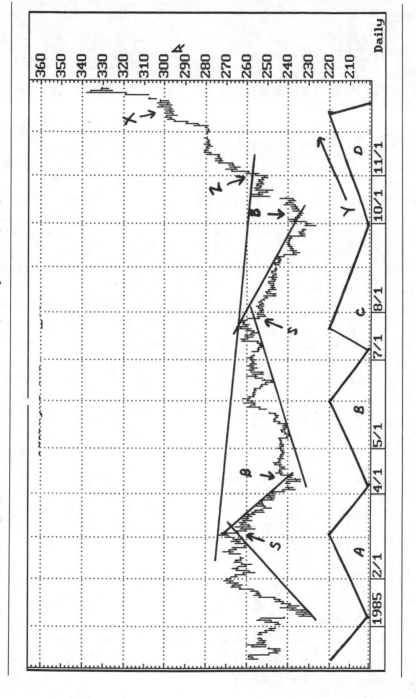

FIGURE 8.11 *Cycle Low in Gold and Trend Line Signals*

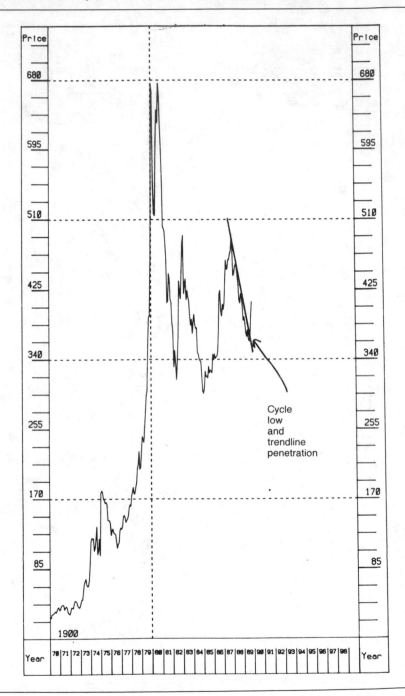

Cycle
low
and
trendline
penetration

stock averages, industry group averages, and cash prices that reflect possible cyclical changes in prices. Cycle lows in gold stocks, for example, can be timed using the cash gold cycles and trend-line signals on the cash gold charts (see figure 8.11).

Trend-Line Channel Analysis and Cycles

Stock prices tend to move in *channels,* price trends bounded by a resistance line above prices and a support line below prices, both moving in the same direction. Figures 8.12 and 8.13 show examples of channels in bull and bear markets, respectively, while figures 8.14 and 8.15 show channels in actual prices.

Aggressive stock traders use channel extremes as buy and sell points during well-defined cyclical trends, buying stocks in a bull market when they fall to the lower channel extreme, taking profits when they rise to their resistance point and buying again when they fall to their support level. This procedure is recommended only when prices are in a cyclical up trend, and only for active traders.

Conversely, the active or aggressive trader sells stocks short in a bear market cycle when prices rise to the upper channel extreme, taking profits when they fall to their support point and selling short again when they rise to their resistance level. This procedure is recommended only when prices are in a cyclical down trend.

Channels, support lines, resistance lines, and breakouts for stock trading are familiar to most investors. Combining these techniques with cycles, however, is new to a majority of investors. With this combined approach you can improve timing and increase the probability that you are investing with the major trend as opposed to fighting the important price trend. Figures 8.16 and 8.17 illustrate the ideal application of this approach in bull and bear markets in combination with cycles.

FIGURE 8.12   *Example of Channel Analysis*

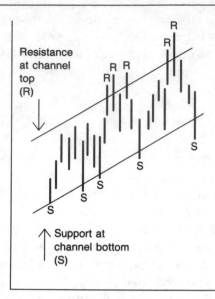

FIGURE 8.13   *Example of Channel Analysis*

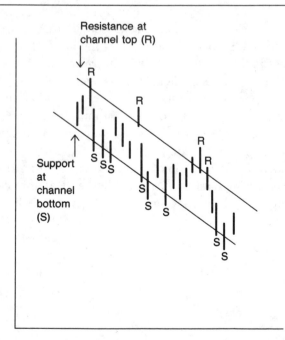

FIGURE 8.14   *Combined Approach to Cycle Timing*

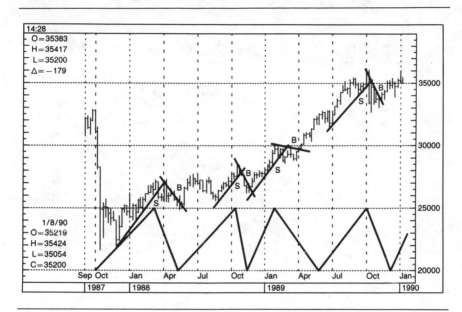

FIGURE 8.15   *Combined Approach to Cycle Timing*

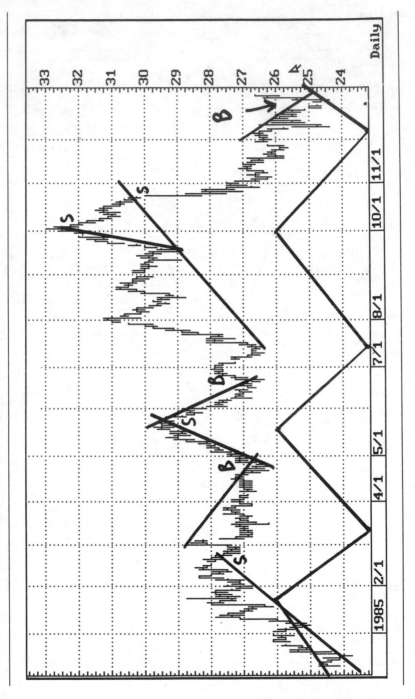

FIGURE 8.16 *Actual Channel in Stocks*

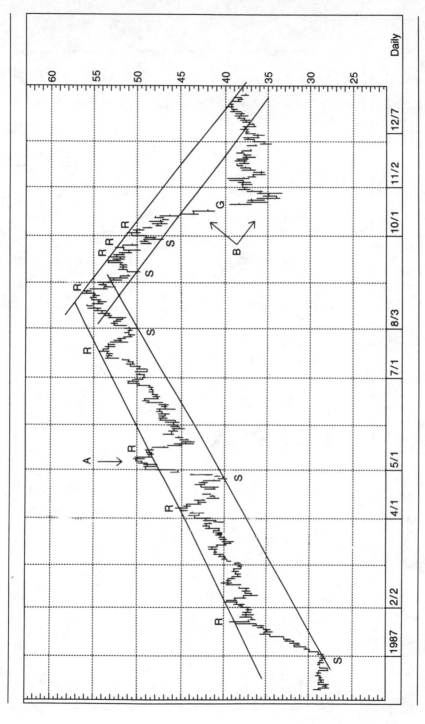

Chart courtesy of Aspen Research

FIGURE 8.17   *Actual Channel in Stocks*

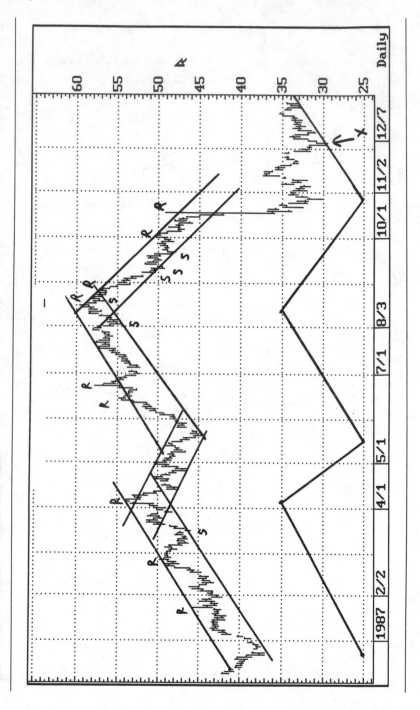

Chapter 9

Advanced Timing I: Moving Averages

An advanced approach to cyclical timing uses *moving averages*—an average of prices that spans a given number of time intervals. In other words, a forty-day moving average of closing prices is simply the last forty days' worth of closing prices added up and divided by forty. Each moving average in the sequence is the most current forty days. As the oldest price is dropped from the calculations, the most current price is added. A moving average smooths price trends by eliminating the effect of price swings that are either far above or below the mean or average.

Stock and futures traders have used moving averages for many years, regardless of the underlying cyclical tendency. Figure 9.1 shows the Standard & Poor's 500 monthly stock average plotted against a twenty-four-month moving average. Penetrations of price above the moving-average line tend to result in continued movement in the direction of the penetration, whereas penetrations below the moving-average line tend to result in continued downward movement.

Now examine the same chart with both the moving average line and the approximate four-year cycle lows shown (figure 9.2). There are fewer false starts for the moving average when the cyclical trend is factored in as a filter for the moving average and vice versa. Moving averages selected for timing purposes typically should be about one-half the length of the cycle being used. Therefore, an approximate four-year or forty-eight-month cycle should be timed with the use of an approximate two-year or twenty-four-month cycle.

Although the single moving-average approach is an effective one, using two moving averages can be more effective, often producing fewer

FIGURE 9.1 *S&P VS 24-Month Moving Average*

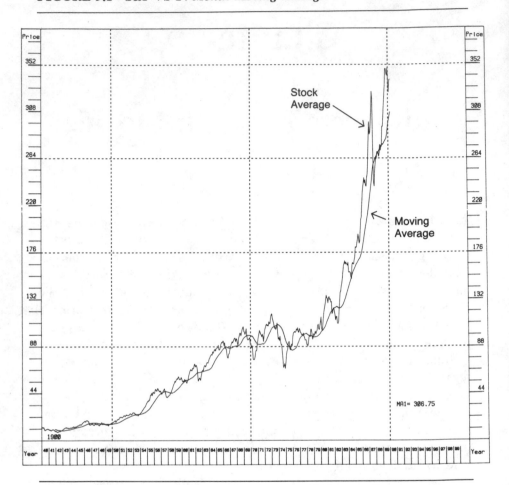

false or losing signals. The combination of two moving averages yields signals as follows:

1. When the shorter of the two moving averages crosses above the longer of the two moving averages, a buy signal is generated.

2. When the shorter of the two moving averages crosses below the longer of the two moving averages, a sell signal is generated.

FIGURE 9.2 *S&P Showing 24-Month M.A. and Four-Year Cycles*

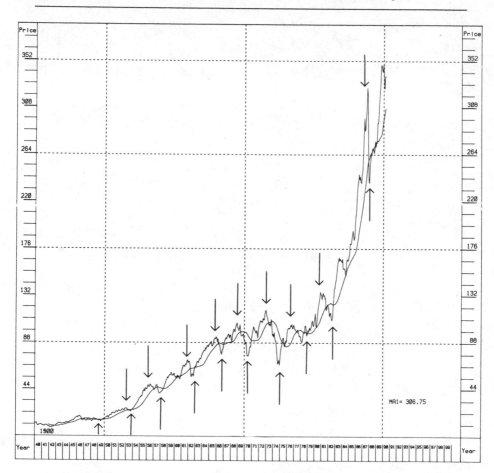

Remember that these signals are to be used in conjunction with cycles in order to improve timing and accuracy. Figures 9.3 and 9.4 illustrate the ideal application of this technique, and figure 9.5 illustrates its actual application. The longer moving average should be about one-half the cycle length, and the shorter moving average should be about one-half the length of the longer moving average.

FIGURE 9.3 *Ideal Sell Signals and Dual M.A.*

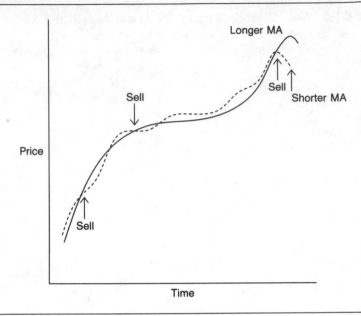

FIGURE 9.4 *Ideal Buy Signals and Dual M.A.*

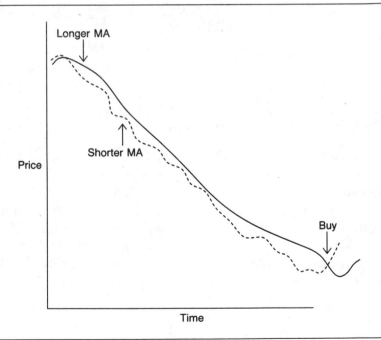

FIGURE 9.5 *Actual Use of Two MA's on Daily Stock Chart*

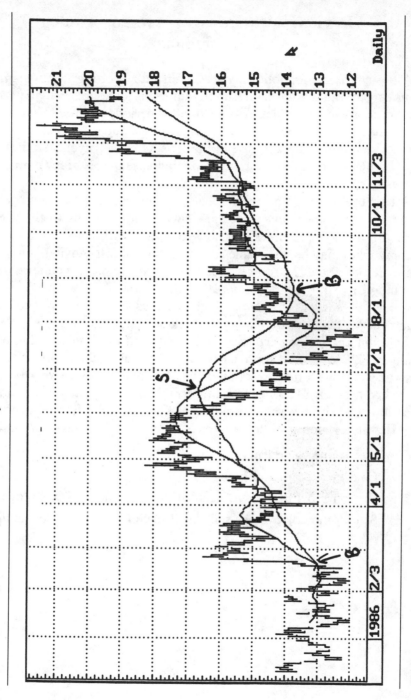

Chart courtesy of Aspen Research

Reviewing the Moving-Average Timing Technique

Although useful for following trends and for spotting trend changes, moving averages often can result in numerous losses, particularly when markets are moving sideways for extended periods of time. The investor who uses only moving averages to generate buy and sell signals in stocks must be willing to accept these limitations. However, cyclical indicators and other timing signals can markedly increase the accuracy of moving averages.

This chapter has covered the basics of moving-average timing. Although there are many more sophisticated approaches to the use of moving averages, complexity is not synonymous with efficacy. Complex approaches may be applicable and necessary in fast-moving, low-margin markets such as futures, but basic indicators, particularly when combined with cycles, are more practical in stock investing.

The advent of affordable, high-powered computer systems has spawned a rash of computerized stock selection and timing systems, including those using artificial intelligence and machine learning techniques. These types of approaches may be useful in stock options analysis or stock index futures trading, but I feel that they are overkill when applied to stock investing. The simple moving average and cycle combinations described herein are sufficient for most investment purposes.

Here is a synopsis of how to use cycles with moving-average timing:

1. Determine cycle length;
2. Find cycle lows and highs;
3. Buy on moving-average signal in time window of cycle law;
4. Sell on moving-average sell-signal in time window of cycle high.

Chapter 10

Moving-Average Channel Technique

Technical market understanding is developed by effective trend analysis. The trend-oriented investor or trader must ask these questions:

1. What is the direction of the current trend?
2. Is there an objective way to determine the existing trend?
3. Where and when did the trend change?
4. How can trend changes be recognized early enough to be used profitably?

The increasing availability of high-powered computers has spawned many variations on the theme of moving averages. I have worked extensively with moving averages of many kinds, including smoothed, exponential, weighted, and displaced. Each approach has its own assets and liabilities, but for many years technical analysts have used only closing prices as their raw data for computing moving averages.

This chapter discusses a more advanced application of the moving-average technique—the moving-average channel (MAC) technique. The MAC can be used as a stand-alone timing system, but the specific money management rules and stop loss procedures needed to be added to the basic timing signals are not covered here since my focus is on cyclical timing methods. As an adjunct to cycles, the MAC technique has especially good potential. The MAC technique can, with further rules, serve as a stand-alone timing system, or it can be used in conjunction with cycles to improve timing.

Thank You, Richard Donchian

The MAC technique was originally proposed by Richard Donchian in the 1950s. Known as the father of moving averages Donchian was

123

responsible for starting a quiet but persistent revolution in technical analysis. Many traders are familiar with Donchian's work with moving averages of closing prices and with his rules for following breakouts, but few traders are acquainted with his high and low moving-average channel work. Instead of plotting only closing price moving averages against prices, Donchian suggested plotting the high and low price moving averages against prices. This approach creates a moving-average band or channel (see figure 10.1).

Examine prices in relation to the MAC as it appears in figure 10.2. Before you read my answers, what conclusions can you reach about the relationship between prices and the MAC? Now study figure 10.3, which shows another stock and its MAC. Have you formulated any conclusions yet? Here are some of my findings:

1. When prices are trending higher, the MAC tends to serve as support. Prices usually bounce back to the upside after they fall into the channel. Investors can buy on declines to the channel, as long as prices have clearly turned higher. Figure 10.4 illustrates this condition.

2. When prices are trending lower, the MAC tends to serve as resistance. When prices rise to the channel, they usually turn lower. Aggressive stock traders can use the channel lines as points to sell stocks short. Figure 10.5 illustrates this condition.

3. When a stock or a stock index shows three consecutive price bars completely above the top of the channel, this usually indicates that an up trend has started; three consecutive price bars below the channel bottom suggest that a down trend has begun. Figures 10.6 and 10.7 illustrate this condition.

As you can see from these illustrations, the MAC can serve as a powerful timing indicator as well as a precise method of determining support and resistance in stock prices. It is uncanny how channel lines frequently serve as support following bearish news in bull markets and how well they halt bear market rallies.

After extensive research and experimentation with different lengths of MAC values, I recommend using a ten-period moving average of high prices and an eight-period moving average of low prices. Empirical testing has shown that since prices tend to fall faster than they rise a shorter moving average of the lows (rather than of the highs) results in a quicker cross of prices below the MAC.

FIGURE 10.1 *A Moving Average High-Low Channel. HMA-10 Week MA of Highs; 8 Week MA of Lows*

Chart courtesy of Aspen Research

How the MAC May Be Used with Cycles

Cycles can be used to fine tune the MAC. Neither the MAC nor cycles are without limitations, but the two approaches combined can yield synergistic results. Here are some suggested applications of the combined approach along with illustrations:

1. When the cycle has turned higher, use the three price bars above the MAC top as a signal to buy. You also can write puts against your long positions, and aggressive traders can buy calls or sell puts. Figures 10.8 and 10.9 illustrate this application.

FIGURE 10.2   *The MAC and Weekly Prices in GE Stock 1982–1989*

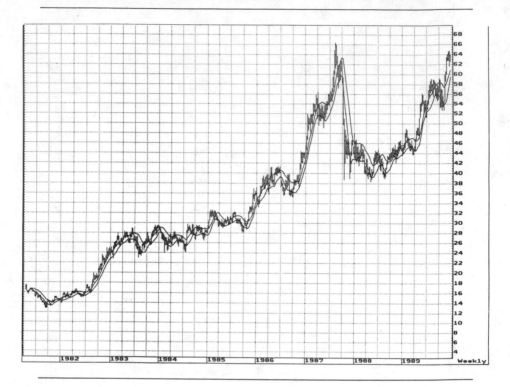

Chart courtesy of Aspen Research

2. When the cycle has turned higher, conservative investors can place GTC orders near the bottom of the channel to go long stocks in the event of a corrective and most likely temporary price reaction. Figures 10.10 and 10.11 illustrate this condition.

3. When the cycle has turned lower, use three price bars below the channel bottom as a signal to either close out long positions or go short. You also can write call options against long stocks, and aggressive traders can buy puts or sell calls. Figures 10.12 and 10.13 illustrate this condition.

4. When the cycle has turned lower and prices have given bearish indications using the MAC, aggressive traders can place GTC orders to go short within the channel. Figures 10.14 and 10.15 illustrate this condition.

FIGURE 10.3 *Daily MAC and Chrysler*

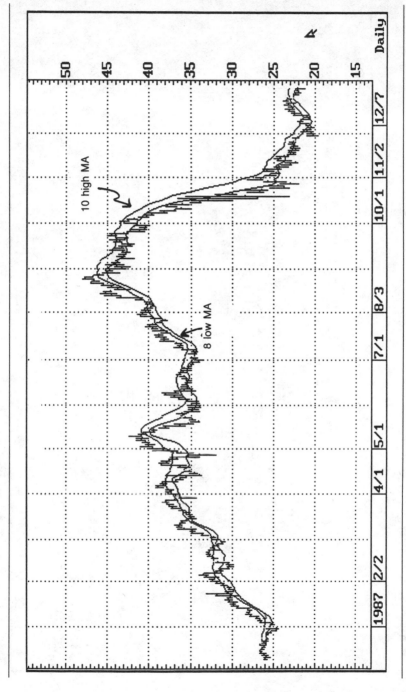

FIGURE 10.4 *Buying at MAC Bottom on Reactions in Bull Market (B = Buy Point)*

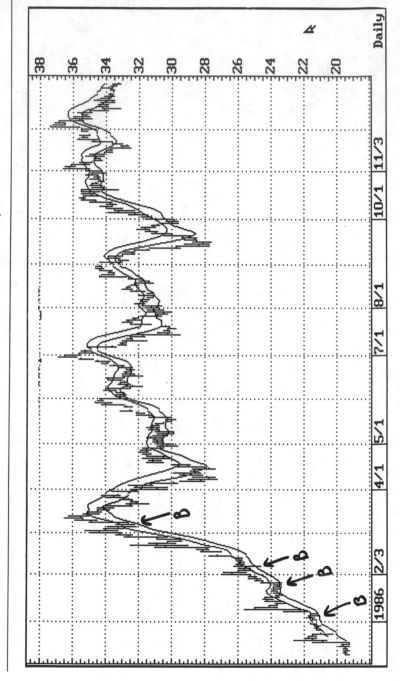

Chart courtesy of Aspen Research

FIGURE 10.5 *Resistance at MAC Top in Downtrends (S = Sell Point)*

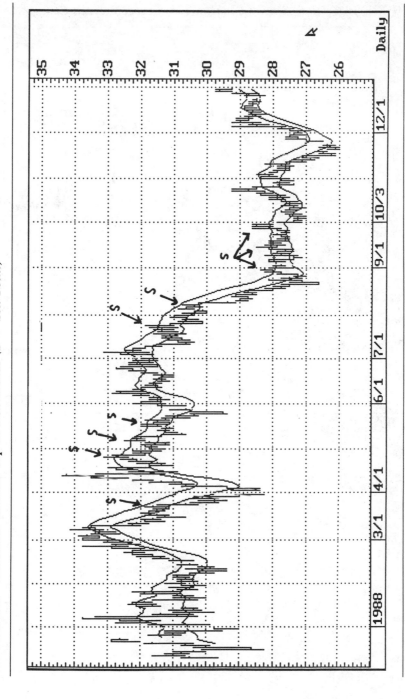

Chart courtesy of Aspen Research

FIGURE 10.6   *Bars Above Channel Signal Probable Trend Change*

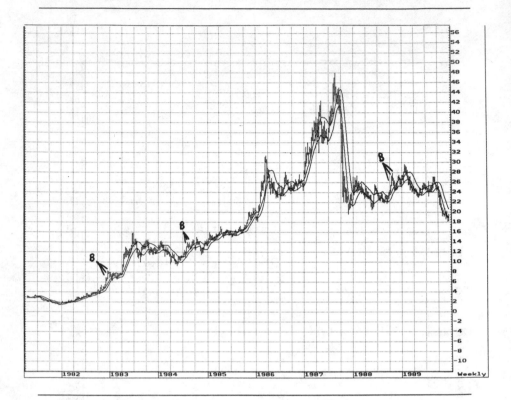

Chart courtesy of Aspen Research

FIGURE 10.7   *Bars Below Channel Signal Probable Trend Change*

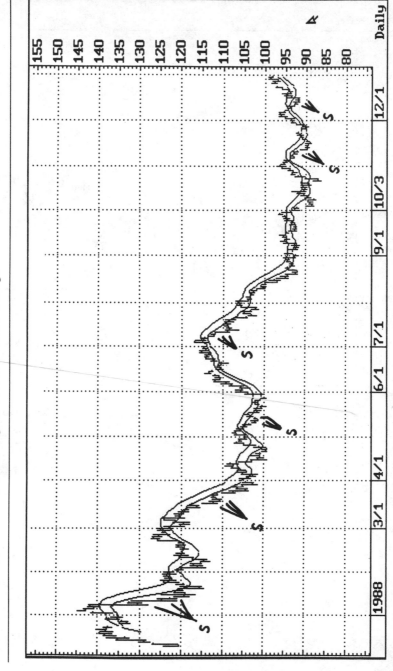

Chart courtesy of Aspen Research

FIGURE 10.8   *Ideal Relationship between Cycle Lows and MAC Buy Signals*

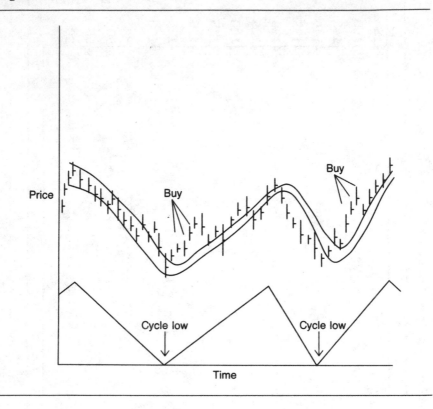

FIGURE 10.9 *Actual Example of MAC Buy Signals and Cycle Low*

Chart courtesy of Aspen Research

FIGURE 10.10   *Ideal Relationship between Cycle Highs and MAC Sell Signals*

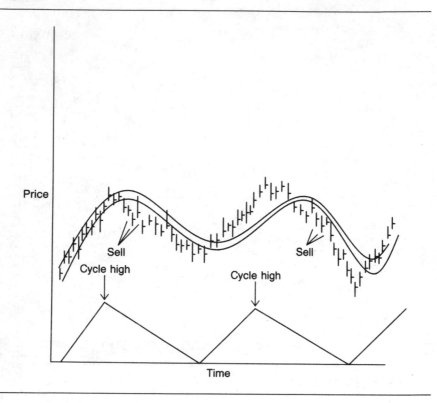

FIGURE 10.11 *Actual Examples of Cycle Tops and MAC Sell Signals*

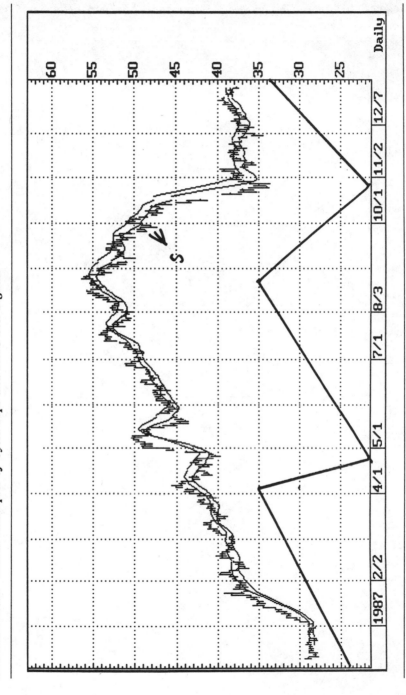

Chart courtesy of Aspen Research

FIGURE 10.12 *Buying on Declines to Channel Support Following Cycle Low; Ideal Example*

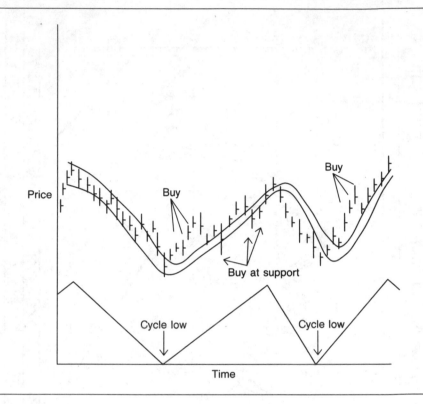

FIGURE 10.13 *Buying on Declines to Channel Support Following Cycle Lows*

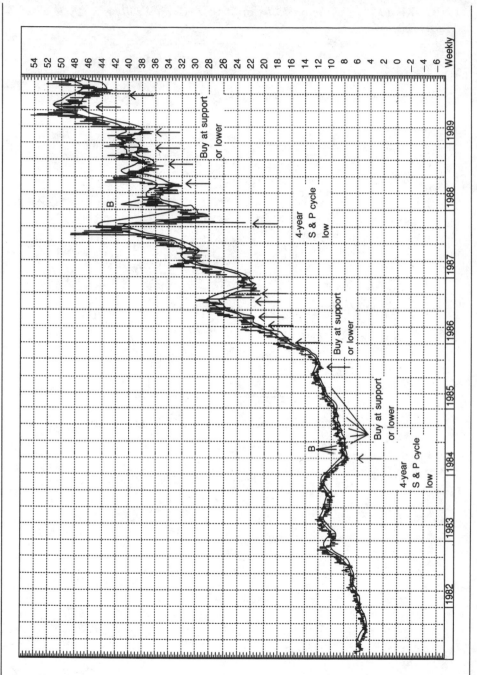

Chart courtesy of Aspen Research

FIGURE 10.14   *Selling on Rally to MAC Resistance following Cycle Top;*
Ideal Example

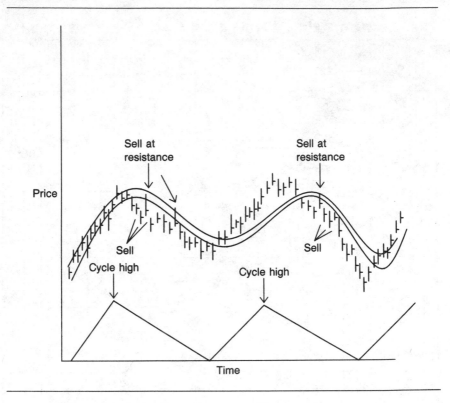

FIGURE 10.15 *Actual Example of Selling at MAC Resistance after Cycle Top*

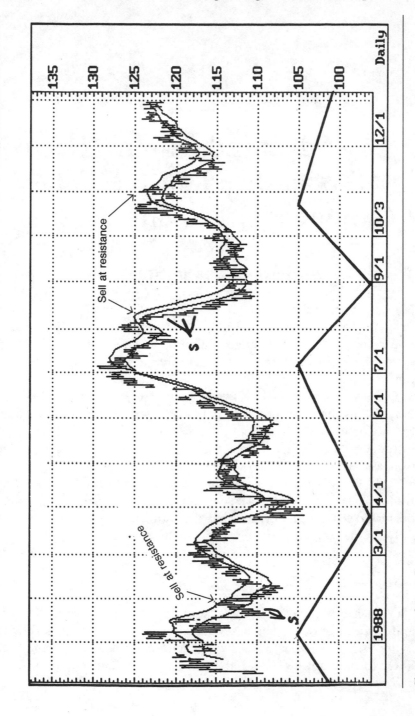

Chart courtesy of Aspen Research

Chapter 11

Advanced Timing II: Stochastics and the Dual Exponential Moving Average

An Introduction to Stochastics

My ongoing search for effective technical trading indicators has led me to study innumerable systems. Over the years the many calls and letters I've received from individuals claiming to have the perfect trading system have convinced me of one fact: the perfect trading system does not exist and never will.

Every so often, though, a technique is developed that has excellent potential as the basis for a wholly new trading system or as an adjunct to an existing trading system. So it is with stochastics. This chapter introduces the concept of stochastics—its basic construction, application, assets, and limitations—and the dual exponential moving average (DEMA) oscillator. The stochastic methodology is not a self-contained trading system, and its use does not guarantee increased profits or decreased losses. The method has limitations. This discussion reflects only my personal adaptation of the technique.

The Basic Stochastic Indicator

The stochastic indicator (SI) consists of two values, percentage of K and percentage of D. The basic application of stochastics is shown in figure 11.1. The indicator tells you when the market is overbought and likely to turn down (80 and above) or oversold and ready to turn up

FIGURE 11.1 *Basic Application of Stochastics*

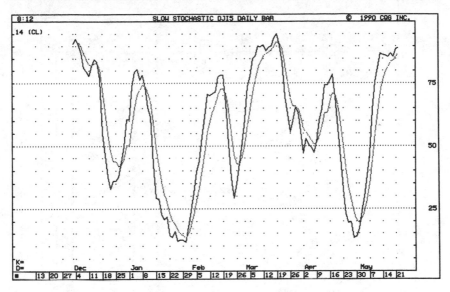

(20 and under). A market does not definitely turn once it enters the critical areas; it must do some price and time work first, and then the SI must turn as well. SI is considered a type of trend-following method because it tends to give signals after tops and bottoms have been made. Figures 11.2 and 11.3 illustrate SI and price relationships. The SI is calculated as follows:

$$Raw \ K_t = [(C_t - L_n)/(H_n - L_n)] \times 100$$
$$\% \ K_t = [(\%K_t - 1 \times 2) + Raw \ K_t]/3$$
$$\%D_t = [(\%D_t - 1 \times 2) + Raw \ K_t]/3$$

where n = number of periods
      t = time
      C = close
      H = High
      L = Low

SI is expressed as two values; %K and %D.

FIGURE 11.2   *Stochastics and Stock Prices*

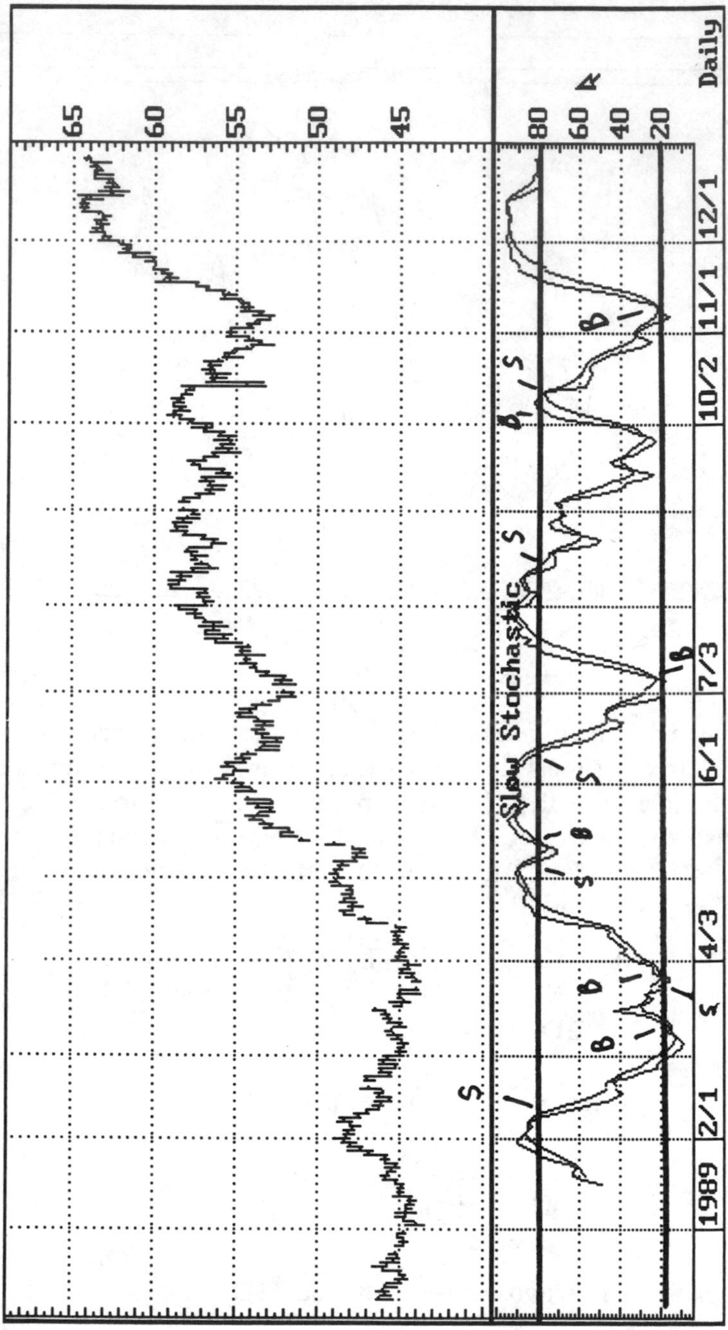

Chart courtesy of Aspen Research

FIGURE 11.3   *Stochastics and Stock Prices*

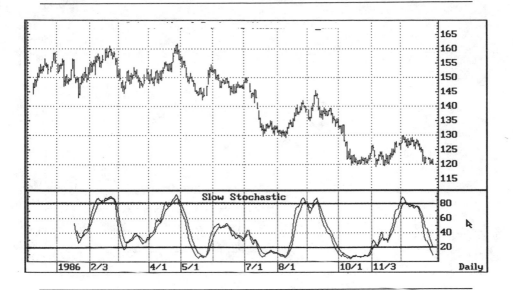

Chart courtesy of Aspen Research

SI Time Frames

The range of SI applications and utility extends from ultra-short-term analysis (that is, five-minute intraday) to monthly analysis. Time frames vary according to individual needs. My preference is for a time segment of twelve to sixteen units, (for example days, weeks, hours). A proper time frame provides a smooth and clear-cut turn. Figures 11.4, 11.5, and 11.6 are daily and weekly charts with various lengths of SI. Examine my notes and comments.

More About the Mathematics of Stochastics

In addition to the basic stochastic indicator formula, the SI may be calculated a number of other ways. Here is my method:

1. Assume you want to run a ten-time-unit SI. Take the highest high and the lowest low of the ten-unit period. Subtract the two.

2. Take the low of the ten units and subtract it from the current close. Divide the difference by the figure arrived at in step 1.

FIGURE 11.4 *Weekly Dow Jones Transportation Index*

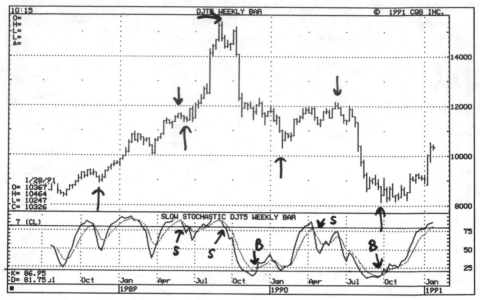

Chart courtesy Commodity Quote Graphics

Note that some cycle tops and bottoms are not necessarily confirmed by stochastic timing.

FIGURE 11.5 *Daily Dow Jones Transportation Index*

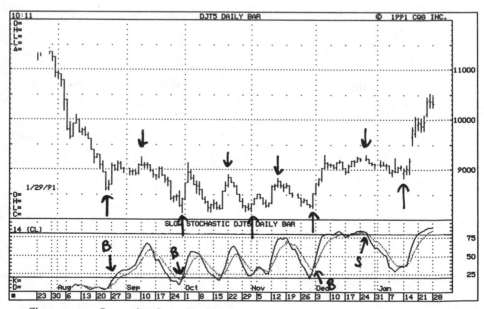

Chart courtesy Commodity Quote Graphics

The arrows show cycle lows and highs. While not all cycle tops and bottoms are accompanied by stochastic signals, other timing indicators, such as moving averages, can be used.

FIGURE 11.6 *Daily Cycles in the Dow Jones Utility Average with Stochastic Signals*

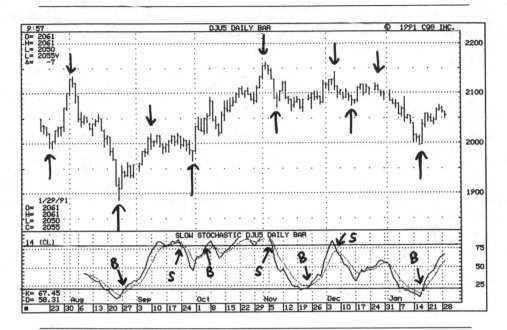

Chart courtesy of Commodity Quote Graphics

3. Drop the oldest data point and recalculate according to steps 1 and 2 using current data, as you would do for a moving average. You have now calculated percentage of K (%K).

4. The second line (called percentage of D, or %D) is a three-period smoothed moving average of the first figure (%K). This completes the calculation for fast stochastic.

5. Slow %K is the fast %D, and slow %D is a three-period smoothed moving average of slow %K.

Limitations of the SI

Perhaps the SI's greatest limitation is that it can give false signals in markets that are very weak or very strong. As the charts in this chapter show (see figure 11.7), it is very possible for the SI to go above 80 and for prices to continue higher while the SI remains above 80 for a

FIGURE 11.7   *Characteristics of SI*

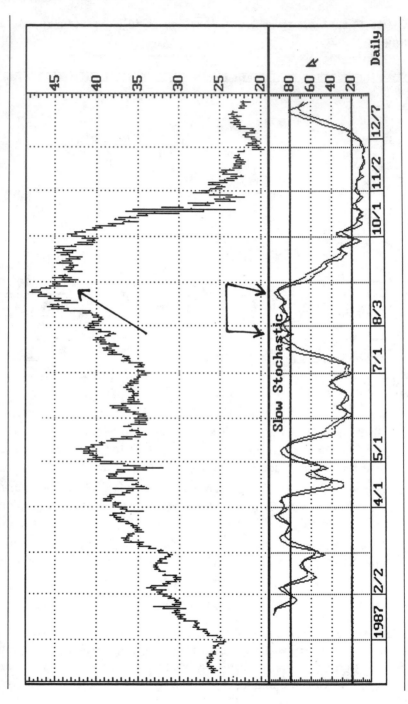

Chart courtesy of Aspen Research

prolonged period. The opposite can happen as well. The trader who continues selling or buying on such extended periods of false signals can run up a considerable string of losses. Some markets can remain over-bought or oversold for days on end.

Another limitation is that the SI does not tell you how much of a move you'll get. When the market is down for an extended period of time, the SI gives an indication to buy, the market rallies only slightly, and before you know it, the SI is overbought. The reverse can happen at bottoms.

Finally, the SI does not help with money management or stops; this must be achieved with other techniques. Generally speaking, it is advisable to use a stop beyond the extreme high or low of the move.

To repeat: the SI works best when used in conjunction with other methods. A computer is not needed unless you want to follow a large number of markets daily, monthly, weekly, and intraday, as I do.

The Dual Exponential Moving Average (DEMA)

The dual exponential moving average (DEMA) consists of two indicators: an oscillator and a moving average of the oscillator. The oscillator is calculated by computing two exponential moving averages and subtracting the smaller from the larger. An exponential moving average of the oscillator is then calculated. The result yields two values. Gerald Appel of Signalert has done considerable work with what he calls moving average convergence/divergence (MACD) (what I call DEMA), particularly in the area of stocks. DEMA, as I use it, can be applied to intraday, daily, weekly, and monthly charts. The basics of the DEMA are simple:

1. The DEMA is a reversing indicator; when a long is closed out a short is established and vice versa, according to the DEMA system.
2. Signals are generated when the two DEMA values cross.

Figure 11.8 is a chart of the DEMA without price. I have marked the buy and sell signals accordingly. Figure 11.9 is the same DEMA plot

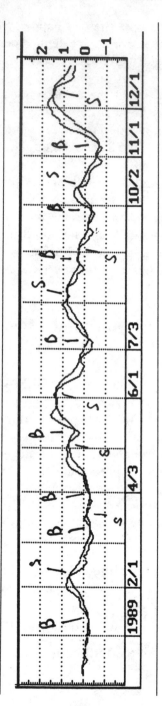

FIGURE 11.8   DEMA Without Price

FIGURE 11.9 *DEMA With Buy/Sell Signals and Cycles*

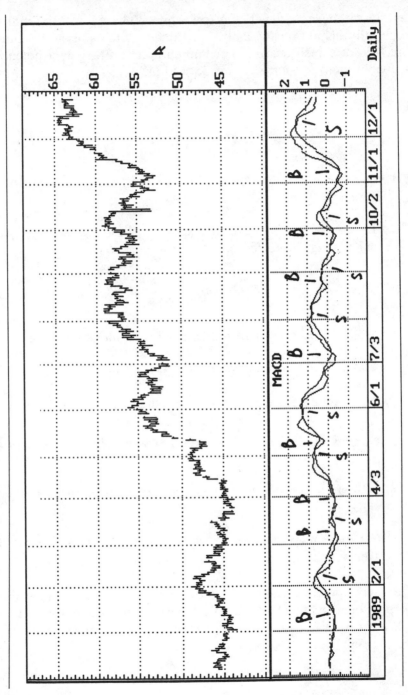

with price above it and with buy/sell signals. I have found this indicator especially helpful on the daily and intraday charts, as well as in the analysis of spread charts. I recommend the DEMA as a potentially valuable tool for optimizing cyclic timing.

Calculations

DEMA can be calculated according to the following formulas and operations:

1. Determine the length of the exponential moving average by first calculating the coefficient using this formula:

$$\text{Coefficient} = \frac{2}{N + 1}$$

   where N = number of time units in the moving average.

2. Compute the moving average (MA) as follows:

Value = (closing price − MA × coefficient) + previous value.

3. Compute the second exponential average, using the same procedure.

4. Subtract the smaller from the larger. This gives you the oscillator value.

5. Calculate an exponential MA of the oscillator. This gives you the average value.

The oscillator and average values are compared with each other for the purpose of generating buy and sell signals. When the average value falls below the oscillator value a sell signal occurs. A buy signal occurs when the average value rises above the oscillator value.

Using the Dual Exponential Moving Average

The DEMA is sensitive to precise values. I use the following values on my quote graphics system: .213 exponential MA, .108 exponential MA, and a .199 exponential MA of the difference of the first two MAs. The result is a two-line indicator that generates buy and sell signals on closing crossovers. Like all timing indicators, however, DEMA is not perfect. When a market has made a sharp move, up or down, the oscillator values tend to signal a turn but the market may fail to respond as expected. In this kind of situation, money management and risk limitation come into play. Figure 11.10 shows the basic signals generated by the DEMA in combination with stochastics, cycles, and traditional trend-line analysis. This combination appears to improve the results of all these indicators.

FIGURE 11.10   *Basic Signals Generated by DEMA*

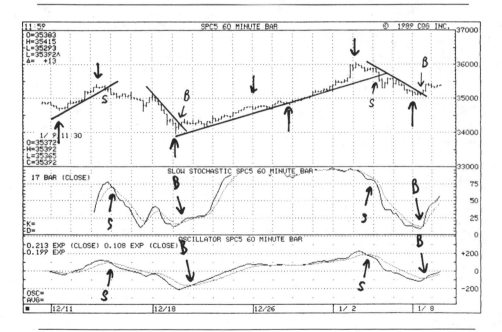

Chart courtesy of Commodity Quote Graphics

Chapter 12

Divergence: The Early Warning Indicator

Divergence is a simple but powerful concept in analysis of stocks and futures. Although it is not used as a timing indicator, it is especially useful as an early warning indicator of either pending strength or weakness in a particular stock or in a given group of stocks.

Divergence occurs when one stock or indicator is moving in a direction contrary to another. If, for example, the Dow Jones industrial average is making a new all-time high but at the same time the Dow transport index is not making a new high, a divergent condition exists. The behavior of a specific stock might diverge from the behavior of its own industry group or from a broad-based average of stock activity. Assume that in a given industry group stocks are moving lower, making new two-year lows, while a specific stock in the given industry group is beginning to move higher. In this case the specific stock is said to show bullish divergence. The assumption is that the stock, which is most likely strong for important fundamental reasons, is being accumulated by sophisticated traders, insiders, or fund managers who expect it to perform well over time. Examples of divergence are shown in figures 12.1 and 12.2.

A classic example of bullish divergence occurred in 1989 between the prices of gold bullion and gold mining shares. Gold prices were in a declining trend for most of 1989, while gold shares, such as Homestake Mining, began to move higher before gold bullion bottomed. This was an early indication that gold shares were likely to become very strong once the price of gold bullion made its low. This was, in fact, the case. When gold finally bottomed, stocks became very strong.

Bearish divergence is also an early warning indicator, suggesting that

153

FIGURE 12.1   *Bullish Divergence: Ideal Example. As price moves down, oscillator moves up, suggesting that a low is due.*

Chart courtesy of Commodity Quote Graphics

the price of a given stock or stock index will move lower because it is not acting in unison with broad-based indicators. The underlying assumption is that large, knowledgeable traders, and insiders are selling the stock in anticipation of a declining trend.

Bearish and bullish divergence are particularly evident at new highs or new lows for a given move or time span. Figures 12.3 and 12.4 illustrate an example of bullish divergence.

Remember that divergence is not a timing indicator but rather merely an early warning sign. It is an advance indication of either distribution (selling) or accumulation (buying) by insiders or other savvy traders. Typically, bullish and bearish divergence are most evident at or near major market turning points such as cyclical highs and lows, but divergence is very much a function of the time frame being used. In other words, you can observe divergence on a daily, weekly, monthly, or an

FIGURE 12.2 *Bearish Divergence: Ideal Example. As DJIA makes new highs, oscillator indicator does not, suggesting a weak market.*

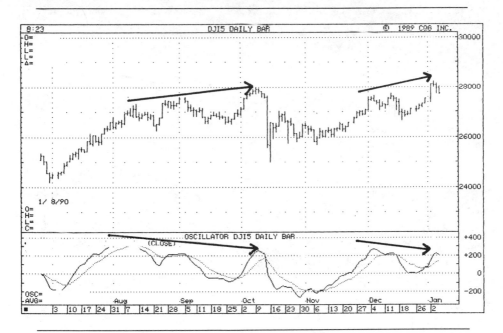

Chart courtesy of Commodity Quote Graphics

intraday basis. Most traders should monitor weekly or monthly divergence. A great deal also can be learned from daily divergence. The combination of cycles and divergence is a very effective tool.

Divergence and Cycle Tops: What to Expect

Because divergence is most likely to be observed at important market turning points, at cyclical tops you can expect to find bearish divergence. Although bearish divergence at or near cyclical tops is not an indication to get out of stocks immediately or to sell stocks short, it is a warning sign that all is not well either with the market or with a

FIGURE 12.3 *Bullish Divergence in Weekly S&P versus Dow Transport Index. Broader based S&P (A) led the way in spite of new low on transport (B).*

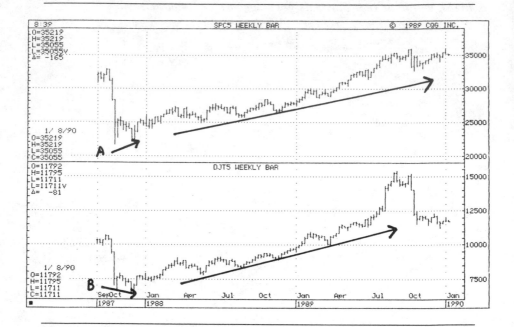

FIGURE 12.4 *Bearish Divergence in GE versus Price Oscillator*

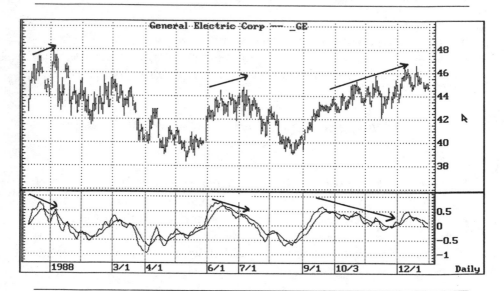

specific stock. Figure 12.5 shows a situation that might develop between a cycle, an oscillator, and a specific stock.

The prudent investor who has accumulated a large amount of stock should watch those stocks closely during the time frame of a cyclical top. If stock averages are making new highs for this move, or if the industry group for your stock is making new highs and your stock is not, then it's probably time to begin selling out some of your position or to enter stop losses to lock in a profit (assuming, of course, that you have one).

Remember that you may not have much time to act. No rule tells us how much advance notice bearish divergence provides; it may give us as much as several months to act or as little as several days. Another point to remember is that bearish divergence does not always occur at bull market tops. When significant bearish divergence occurs on a daily or an intraday basis, it may not be visible on weekly or monthly charts, which are, as a function of their time span, less sensitive to relatively brief technical developments.

Divergence and Cycle Bottoms: What to Expect

At cyclical bottoms expect to find bullish divergence. Although bullish divergence at or near cyclical bottoms is not an indication to get out of short positions immediately or to buy stocks, it is a warning sign that a bottom may be forming in the market or in a specific stock. Figure 12.6 shows a situation that might develop between a cycle, an oscillator, and a specific stock at a cyclical bottom.

As with cyclical tops, the prudent investor who has accumulated a large short position should watch those stocks closely during the time frame of a cyclical bottom. If stock averages are making new lows for this move, or if the industry group for your stock is making new lows and your short positions are not, then it's probably time to begin buying frame of a cyclical bottom. If stock averages are making new lows for this move, or if the industry group for your stock is making new lows and your short positions are not, then it's probably time to begin buying back some of your position or to enter stop losses to lock in a profit (assuming, of course, that you have one).

FIGURE 12.5 *Cycle Tops and Bearish Divergence in Disney*

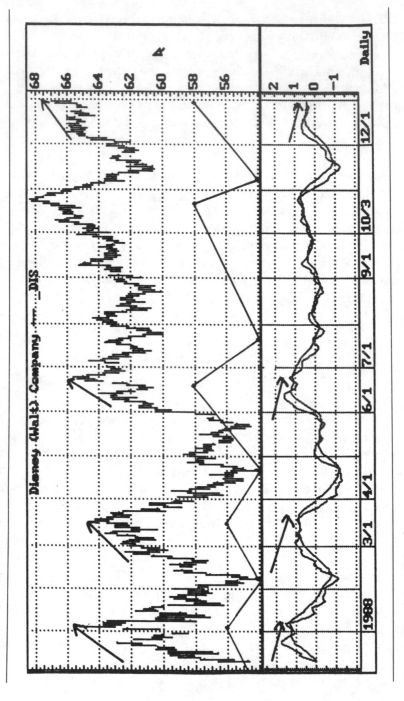

Chart courtesy of Aspen Research

FIGURE 12.6   *Bullish Divergence at Four-Year Cycle Low*

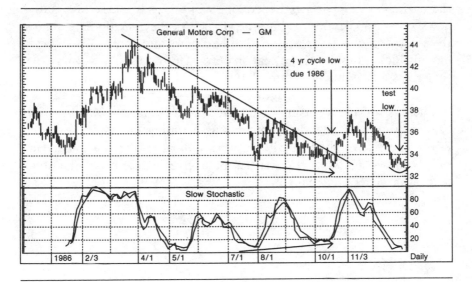

Chart courtesy of Aspen Research

Once again, you may not have much time to act. Bullish divergence may give several months to act or only give us several days. Remember also that bullish divergence does not always occur at bear market bottoms. Significant bullish divergence on a daily or an intraday basis may be obscured on weekly or monthly charts.

Divergence and the News Backdrop

A less formal approach to divergence is the relationship between political and economic news and market trends. Have you noticed that stocks tend to move down on good news and up on bad news? Have you seen stocks reach major peaks coincident with exceptionally positive news and major bottoms on exceptionally bearish news?

Indeed, stocks tend to anticipate the news. Consider a prime example of bullish divergence between price and news. When a given industry group or a given stock is bearish, and when the news backdrop is also negative, knowledgeable investors may be looking beyond the current news. They may be aware of a pending improvement in the business of the particular company and therefore will take advantage of negative news as an opportunity to buy the stock. As they accumulate shares, the stock becomes less responsive to bad news and actually may begin moving higher in spite of the bearish news. This is an early warning sign that the stock is under accumulation and likely to soon turn higher, possibly for an extended length of time.

There is no rule for using divergence in combination with the news backdrop or with new developments as a timing indicator, however. Divergence is simply an early warning indicator that the underlying supply and demand characteristics of a given stock or of the stock market in general is changing.

Chapter 13

Forecasting Stock Cycles: Blessing or Curse?

Cyclical analysis can be a valuable tool in forecasting stock cycles, but any forecasts must be validated by one or more timing indicators such as moving averages and trend-line breakout signals.

Forecasting does have its potential dangers and pitfalls. To avoid them, it is necessary to remember that the goals of a forecaster are distinctly different from those of a speculator or an investor. The forecaster's task—correctly predicting the future—is less difficult than the the investor's and even less difficult than the immense effort required of the speculator.

Romance versus Pragmatism

Forecasting the probable direction of stocks, the stock market, or the economy is exciting. For thousands of years humankind has been fascinated with predicting future events, turning to all manner and sorts of techniques for doing so. When shelter and food are primary concerns, as they were with early hunters and gatherers, being able to shine even the smallest light into the immediate future constitutes a potentially significant tool for survival. By observing winds, animal behavior, the moon, the sun, and the stars prehistoric peoples were able to forecast with considerable accuracy those things that concerned them the most—the weather, the availability of food, and the approach of enemies.

Today we don't need to forecast the weather; others do it for us. If we have money, we can buy our next meal. As humans learned to satisfy their primary needs, their need to see into the future became more focused on abstractions and complex combinations of events. Will tomorrow bring a nuclear war? How will the next presidential election turn out, and what effects will it have on domestic and international economics? Which way will interest rates move?

Forecasting the future is as important today as it was thousands of years ago. People today are just as concerned with survival as were people of earlier times. We face many of the same challenges and devote intense efforts to developing computer models that will forecast economic trends.

But forecasting cannot necessarily bring us any closer to success in any particular field. A forecast is merely an attempt to predict the future based on what has happened in the past. All forecasts and models are based on historical behavior, relationships, and if/then statements. Forecasts are not always right and, in fact, are often wrong at critical points.

To a great extent, forecasting is a romantic pursuit. Despite the mystique that surrounds forecasting, however, an excellent forecaster is not necessarily a successful investor or speculator. Success in the area of investing requires more diverse skills than does forecasting. Although modern methods of forecasting are complex, they are not as concerned with pragmatics. The forecaster may make an accurate prediction but not be concerned with what transpired between the time that the forecast was made and the time that the actual event occurred. Investors and speculators, on the other hand, must live with their investments every day and are subject to the news, margin calls, financial demands, fear, greed, and a host of other subtle and not so subtle influences, all of which can affect their actions. Although a forecaster may correctly predict that XYZ Company stock will rise from $10 today to $40 in three years, the stock may drop to $2 first and possibly force the investor to liquidate the shares. Perhaps the stock may rise to $25 quickly and the investor may decide to add shares at this price. The stock might then drop to $9, forcing the investor to close out the position for fear of a further drop.

As you can see, forecasting and investing or speculating are entirely different matters. Access to excellent forecasts does not guarantee successful investing. In fact, in the short run, forecasting may result in overconfidence, overcommitment of funds, and a loss before the forecast events occur. Good timing and risk management remain integral parts of the equation for success.

Forecasting and Human Psychology

Human beings are hopeful creatures indeed. We pray for world peace. We hope that the future will be better than the present or the past. And we wish to achieve financial success. In order to achieve success in the world of investing and speculating—whether in stocks, real estate, or futures trading—you must learn to follow trends, avoid opinions, and deal with the reality of the markets. Anything less will prove costly. To achieve consistent success in stocks you must learn the following:

1. Develop and form attitudes and opinions about the markets and about stocks.
2. Ignore information that is not derived from your own method of analysis.
3. Critically evaluate and thoroughly examine the information you do accept from other sources prior to acting on this information.
4. Be as unemotional as possible about investments.
5. Follow trends and avoid forecasts as much as possible.

To forecast a trend or price is to set up an expectation—in fact, a goal—and human beings work toward goals. Although an admirable objective in life, working toward a goal may prove to be a detriment in the world of investing.

Consider the significant difference between buying a stock because you expect it to go up and buying a stock because you expect it to go to $120 per share by next year. Buying a stock with the expectation that it will rise is reasonable. Protection in the form of a stop loss virtually guarantees an acceptable loss if the expectation is wrong. Buying a stock in the expectation of a rise to $120 leaves the investor with a specific expectation, and the expectation may cause the investor to ignore money management rules, holding the stock as it moves all the way back down to, perhaps even lower than, the original entry price because of the expectation that a move to $120 per share was almost certain. It takes a disciplined investor to know how a forecast may be properly used. In this case a trailing stop loss order should have been used regardless of the forecast.

One way to avoid this problem is to follow rather than forecast trends. When a cycle low has developed and timing indicators add to the certainty that a low is in place, the trend is said to have turned higher, and long positions are in order. The trend is then followed with appropriate action until the trend changes. When it has, the astute investor changes direction as well, liquidating stocks and perhaps selling short, consistent with the new trend. By following the trend and avoiding a forecast, the investor avoids becoming too emotionally attached to the forecast. When a stock begins its move higher, there is no certain way to tell how high it will go; and when a stock begins its declining cycle there's no certain way to tell how low the stock will go. Cyclical analysis teaches us that "If the time is right, then the price must be right, regardless of what that price may be"!

Chapter 14

Finding Cycles

Computer technology and advanced programming have made the once difficult task of finding cycles considerably less taxing. Although cyclical analysts once relied on observation, visual inspection, and lengthy mathematical investigations to uncover cycles, the task facing contemporary analysts and investors is not to find cycles but rather to choose which cycles to follow. The current status of cyclical analysis in stock prices owes much of its success to the Foundation for the Study of Cycles, where research has been conducted since the 1950s.

As research and practice have become highly specialized, precisely focused computer software has been developed in fields as diverse as music, medicine, accounting, and cyclical analysis. Using techniques such as spectral analysis and Fourier analysis statisticians and mathematicians have been able to isolate literally hundreds of correlations, relationships, patterns, and cycles in widely diverse data bases. By the late 1980s a computer program could "learn" from its data analyses, thereby discovering relationships among the data and formulating rules by various inferential techniques.

As you probably can see, the investor who seeks to discover new cycles in stock prices is embarking on a great adventure in reinventing the wheel. Although the trip may prove enjoyable and the exercise may be good for the mind, investment efforts should be directed at developing a personal investment strategy rather than searching out new cycles. Join the Foundation for the Study of Cycles or purchase any of several computer programs and historical data bases that are designed to help you find cycles; they will make the most economical use of your time and effort.

Familiar stock market cycles may be modified in time, and new cycles may be discovered. Nevertheless, one of the best ways to find cycles is to reap the benefits of someone else's work. Don't spend your time poring over charts attempting to fit cycles into the data. Instead, find a good service or computer program that does the work for you. This is the single best way to find cycles.

If you need to know more about how cycles are found before you can have confidence in the cycles that you are following, however, or if you're the kind of person who needs to know more about the basics of cyclical analysis in order to know how much confidence you can have in a particular service, market analyst, or computer program, then the following very general discussion may prove valuable.

Cycle and Trend

The key issue in cyclical analysis involves the separation of cycles from other cycles. The current trend of a stock or the stock market consists of many cyclical components, all operating with varying degrees of influence at the same time. By extracting as many of the cyclical components from the data series investors can examine each cycle, determining its role, importance, and future direction. Then the cycles can be reconstructed into a forecast or extrapolation that should bear close resemblance to actual events. Because it is not possible to know all of the cyclical influences affecting stock prices, we cannot reconstruct reality or forecast it with 100 percent accuracy. This problem is alleviated by the use of timing indicators. In the field of cyclical analysis, however, there are purists who seek to refine techniques to their highest possible degree of accuracy. Technology will improve techniques of cyclical analysis and forecasting and eventually may reach a level of sophistication that allows for highly accurate forecasting. I maintain that the tools for generating such forecasts will become widely available, the markets will become more efficient, and the system will become so highly predictable that it ultimately becomes less predictable.

The task of separating cycles from other cycles is a formidable one. Perhaps the simplest approach, and the one used by analysts for many years, is that of visual inspection. Many, such as the approximate four- and eight-year stock market cycles, are clearly visible. Although the actual length of each cycle can vary, at times considerably, timing can minimize the degree of error due to such fluctuations.

Detrending

Perhaps one of the most basic techniques for finding cycles is to detrend the raw data. This approach involves the following steps:

1. Construct a simple moving average of prices.
2. Subtract each price from the moving average.
3. Plot the difference derived from step 2 against actual prices.
4. The new, detrended data will display the cycles, and the detrended data will be related to actual cyclical highs and lows in the raw data.

As an example, consider figures 14.1 through 14.4, which show the Dow Jones industrial average detrended for four different moving-average lengths in order to make the cycles more visible. This very basic approach can be used by many traders with minimal effort and elementary mathematical skills. By taking another step you can convert the detrended moving average into a cyclical timing indicator. All you need to do is to construct a second moving average, which is a moving average of the first moving average. In so doing you've smoothed the data even further, converting the detrended moving average into a timing tool. This approach has considerable merit because of its accuracy and its simplicity. Detrending can make cycles more observable and help time market entry. Additional examples are provided in figures 14.5 and 14.6.

Other Methods

Some of the more advanced methods of cyclical timing include such highly mathematical techniques as spectral analysis, Fourier analysis, and the many variations on their themes. I do not recommend you use them unless you are familiar with higher mathematics and unless you have access to a computer. As I noted earlier, the Foundation for the Study of Cycles is an excellent, economical source for up-to-date information on stocks cycles and cyclical research, including historical data for stock research and various computer programs for cyclical analysis.

FIGURE 14.1   *Daily DJIA Showing Detrended Cycles (Arrows show cycle lows and highs)*

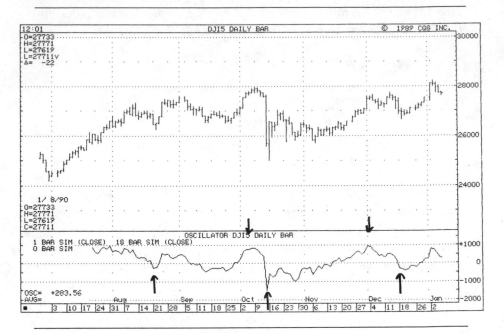

Chart courtesy of Commodity Quote Graphics

Prominent Stock Market Cycles

The following cycles are prominent in the stock market: 9.2 year, 3–4 years, 48 months, 14–19 weeks, 50–60 days, 26–32 days, 19–23 days, and 14 days.

FIGURE 14.2 *Daily DJIA Showing Detrended Cycles for Shorter Term Cycle Lengths*

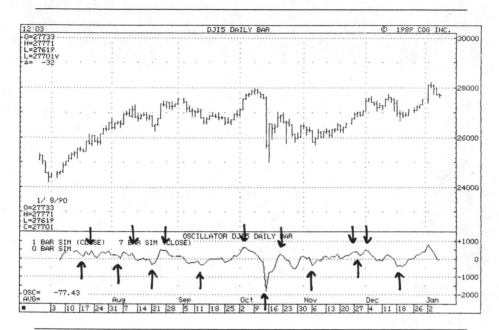

Chart courtesy of Commodity Quote Graphics

FIGURE 14.3 *Weekly DJIA Showing Detrended Cycles*

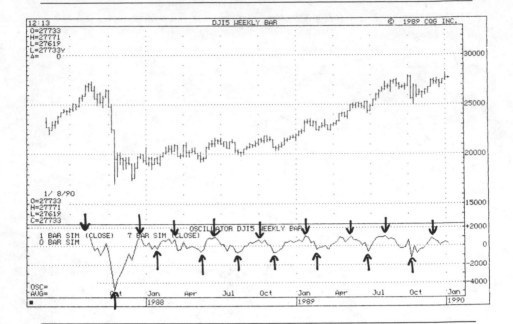

FIGURE 14.4 *Weekly DJIA Showing Detrended Cycles*

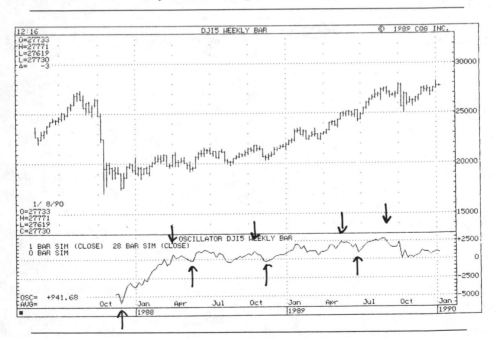

Charts courtesy of Commodity Quote Graphics

FIGURE 14.5 *Daily DJIA Showing Detrended Cycles*

FIGURE 14.6 *Weekly DJIA Showing Detrended Cycles*

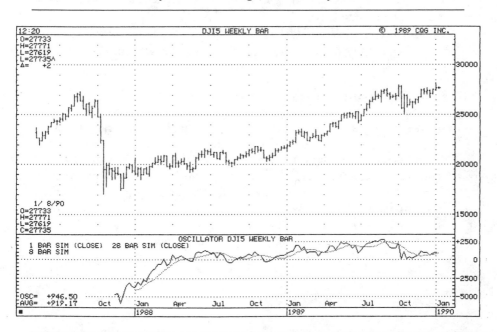

Charts courtesy of Commodity Quote Graphics

Chapter 15

Cycles and Market Sentiment

The history of stock prices is intimately related to mass psychology and human emotion. There is an almost linear relationship between the intensity and consensus of public opinion and major turning points in stock prices. Emotion reigns supreme at significant market turns: fear and negative sentiment correlate highly with market bottoms, and euphoria correlates highly with market tops. Even the most inexperienced investor, however, realizes that exceptionally strong emotions are often inversely correlated with investment success. The more logical and calculating you play the investment game, therefore, the more likely you are to make educated and intelligent decisions, particularly at critical market junctures.

H. M. Gartley, in his classic 1935 book *Profits in the Stock Market,*[1] shares his hard-learned experiences with investor psychology and sentiment:

> Previously, we have stated that stock prices tend to follow, or move coincidentally with the trends of trade and industry. Also, it has been pointed out that upon many occasions, the market tends to discount economic changes. In addition, it has been stated that there are psychological elements within the market, other than purely fundamental causes which relate to economic changes and the earning power of corporations.
>
> Stated in other words we may say that there is a speculative force always present in the market, representing the efforts of those interested in security price trends to discount fundamental changes which they believe are occurring. Mob psychology is also a factor with which to be reckoned. This shows itself best in the fact that, as a general proposition,

---

1. Gartley, H. M., *Profits in the Stock Market* (Greenville SC.: Traders Press, 1935), 8.

the vast number of people interested in stock prices, are constitutionally bullish,—optimists. To them, the up side is the only side.

But Gartley is not alone in his emphasis on the value of emotional self-discipline. Chapter 16 explores investor psychology, but this chapter examines some specific ways in which market consensus can be used to your advantage during the time frame of cyclical turns. It begins with a very basic assumption—namely, that most investors and analysts are incorrect about the direction of stock prices at or near major turning points.

Several hundred years of economic and stock market history have shown that the majority opinion is usually incorrect at important market tops and bottoms. Gartley (1935: 8, 180–181) appreciated this aspect of market sentiment and psychology:

Basically, the primary forces of the market might be designated as:

1. The greed for profits, and
2. The fear of losses.

The action of these forces coupled with the common human trait of going to excesses alternately causes errors of optimism and errors of pessimism to be registered in the price trend.

Thus arises the old Wall Street axiom that "The public gets in at the top, and gets out at the bottom." The public is here defined as—the mass of persons of moderate means,—who take a small interest in the market.

The rise in stock prices in the last quarter of 1928, and the first three quarters of 1929 is an excellent example of an error of optimism carried to the nth degree; while conversely the decline from May to July 1932 is one of the best examples in history, of an error of pessimism. These illustrations apply to the primary trends (bull and bear markets). The same type of phenomenon is occurring constantly in the smaller movements of the market.

Thus, we may depend upon the fact that any substantial rise will be followed by a decline of some extent, which might be termed the correction of part or all of the error of optimism. Conversely, any extended decline, we may expect, will be followed by some kind of an advance, correcting the error of pessimism. It is because so many persons who try to make money in the stock market are either ignorant, or refuse to recognize the importance of these fundamental facts that buying at the top or selling at the bottom is so often the usual procedure.

I sometimes think that speculation must be an unnatural sort of business, because I find that the average speculator has arrayed against him his own nature. The weaknesses that all men are prone to are fatal to success in speculation—usually those very weaknesses that make him likable to his fellows or that he himself particularly guards against in those other ventures of his where they are not nearly so dangerous as when he is trading in stocks or commodities.

The speculator's chief enemies are always boring from within. It is inseparable from human nature to hope and to fear. In speculation when the market goes against you you hope that every day will be the last day—and you lose more than you should had you not listened to hope— to the same ally that is so potent a success-bringer to empire builders and pioneers, big and little. And when the market goes your way you become fearful that the next day will take away your profit, and you get out—too soon. Fear keeps you from making as much money as you ought to. The successful trader has to fight these two deep-seated instincts. He has to reverse what you might call his natural impulses. Instead of hoping he must fear; instead of fearing he must hope. He must fear that his loss may develop into a much bigger loss, and hope that his profit may become a big profit. It is absolutely wrong to gamble in stocks the way the average man does.

Let me review for you the facts we will attempt to use to our advantage before applying specific techniques to stock selection:

1. At major cyclical turning points in individual stock prices and stock averages public and professional sentiment tends to run high. Most analysts, experts, investors, politicians, and the media agree about the probable direction of prices.

2. At cyclical tops these groups are bullish, optimistic, and even euphoric. Problems are downplayed. The underlying economic trend is considered healthy and positive, and the long-term outlook for stock prices is bullish, following, of course, "natural corrections" to the downside.

3. At tops outrageously bullish forecasts predominate for the Dow Jones averages: stocks should double or even triple over the coming years, for example, or all-time highs are not far off. The question is not whether stocks will continue higher or not but how high they will climb and how soon.

4. There is a strong correlation between the bullish sentiment of smaller investors and the timing of major tops. The more bullish the small investor, the more likely the market is near a significant top in prices.

5. Negative news, poor earnings, and unhealthy economic developments tend to evoke only ephemeral declines in stock prices. In fact, following the release of such news prices usually reverse an initial decline as bullish investors consider the drop an opportunity to buy more stock.

6. At cyclical bottoms the consensus of market sentiment of most participants and outsiders is bearish and pessimistic. Problems are considered major and perhaps even terminal. The underlying economic trend is considered unhealthy and deteriorating, and the long-term outlook for stock prices is bearish following, of course, "minimal corrections" to the upside.

7. At bottoms outrageously bearish forecasts dominate the Dow Jones averages: analysts may say that stocks should lose a substantial percentage of their value over the coming years, for example, and that as the economy continues to deteriorate, so will stocks. The question is not whether stocks will continue lower or not but how low they will drop and how soon.

8. There is a strong correlation between the bearish sentiment of smaller investors and the timing of major bottoms. The more bearish the small investor, the more likely the market is near a significant bottom in prices.

9. Bullish news, improved earnings, and positive economic developments tend to evoke only ephemeral rallies in stock prices. In fact, following the release of such news prices usually reverse an initial rally as bearish investors consider the rally an opportunity to sell more stock.

The balance of this chapter provides some ideas about how the average investor can use these underlying principles of market sentiment in timing stock market transactions consistent with the cycles.

Odd Lot Short Sales

One good way to apply these principles to market timing is to monitor odd lot short sales. Keep a close watch on the following relationships between odd lot short sales and cycles:

1. At or near a major cycle low expect to see odd lot short sales increase significantly. A brief but large jump in odd lot short sales suggests that the public has turned negative on the market. When this occurs at or near an anticipated cyclical low, particularly following a sustained downtrend during which odd lotters have been relatively quiet or even bullish, it strongly suggests that a major low has been reached.

2. At or near a major cycle top expect to see odd lot short sales drop significantly. A brief but large decline in odd lot short sales suggests that the public has turned bullish on the market. When this occurs at or near an anticipated cyclical top, particularly following a sustained uptrend during which odd lotters have been relatively quiet or even bearish, it strongly suggests that a major top has been reached.

A number of chart services monitor odd lot short sales (OLSS) regularly and have charted the OLSS ratio for many years. It is a good idea to look at OLSS figures regularly, but particularly during the time frame of a cycle top or bottom. Remember that odd lotters are not always wrong, but they tend to be wrong at major cyclical lows and highs.

Daily Market Sentiment

Although odd lot short sales can help you determine public sentiment on a long-term basis, the daily market sentiment can help you time cyclical trades on a much shorter-term basis. A service that I provide, the Daily Sentiment Index, monitors market sentiment on a daily basis after market closings. I have found the DSI to be an excellent measure of market sentiment for short-term cyclical timing. Figures 15.1 through 15.4 show how daily market sentiment and the daily price of

FIGURE 15.1 *Daily Sentiment Index and Stocks*

FIGURE 15.2 *Daily Sentiment Index and Stocks*

Charts courtesy of Commodity Quote Graphics

FIGURE 15.3 *Daily Sentiment Index and Stocks*

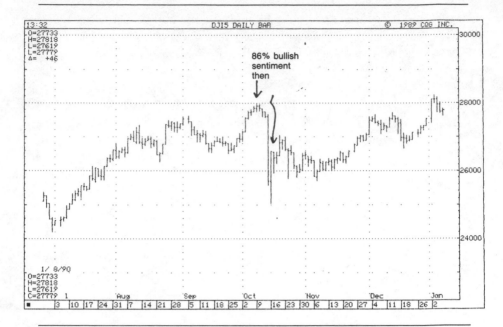

FIGURE 15.4 *Daily Sentiment Index and Stocks*

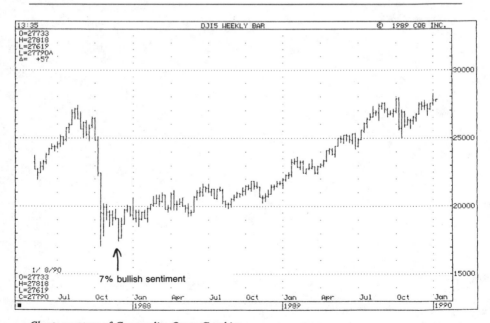

Charts courtesy of Commodity Quote Graphics

stock index futures have been related. As the figures show, extremely low bullish sentiment readings tend to correlate highly with market bottoms, and extremely high bullish sentiment readings tend to correlate highly with market tops.

The Daily Sentiment Index (DSI) is an informational service for futures traders. Based upon the ideas of contrary opinion, the DSI is designed to provide daily bullish sentiment percentages on all active futures markets. Subscribers to the DSI are provided with a daily hotline tape, after market closings, which reports the percentage of bullish sentiment as assessed by our staff. Individuals whose opinions are recorded as either bullish, bearish, or "no comment", are referred to as our "correspondents" or "respondents". In order to maintain a statistically random and representative base of opinion, our correspondents are drawn from every walk of futures life, and from every part of the United States.

Theory and Application of the Daily Sentiment Index

The quintessential aspect of DSI theory is that on any given day a high level of bullish or bearish sentiment, as determined by our survey, is likely to signal a market move in the opposite direction over the next several days, most likely sooner rather than later. Generally speaking, when correspondents are in 75% bullish agreement, or sentiment, there is reason to believe that a market turn to the down will occur very soon. Conversely, when correspondents are in 75% agreement that a bearish move will take place (i.e. 25% or less bullish), then it is likely that a bullish move will take place very soon. It is the nature of contrary opinion indicators to make assumptions that high levels of agreement at the same point in time will likely signal a market move in the opposite direction. In the stock market, for example, analysts closely watch Odd Lot Short Sales figures. These figures determine how much short selling is done by small (supposedly unsophisticated) traders (i.e. odd lotters), who cannot afford to sell short 100 shares of a stock or more. Hence, they sell short in "odd lots" (number of shares less than 100). Generally, when odd lotters are heavy sellers, there is reason, based on historical precedent, to expect a market upmove. When odd lotters are inactive and their short selling is very low, there may be reason to expect a market top. Various sentiment indicators are tracked by traders in stocks and futures. Although techniques of assessment, data gathering, sample type and size vary, the general concept is similar—namely, when opinions are in strong agreement, price trend is likely to turn in the direction opposite from the sentiment.

Application of the DSI percentages is an individual matter. We, at DSI have our favorite applications, but they're not necessarily right for everyone. In order to make effective use of the DSI, the following suggestions may be helpful.

1. Observe the percentages daily for several weeks.
2. Highlight (on your daily recording sheet) the high (75% and over) and low (25% and under) percentages.
3. Observe price behavior in the markets on the next day and for several days thereafter.
4. Watch for price moves opposite from the extreme sentiment readings. In other words, when DSI is 75% or over, watch for a downmove the next several days, most likely the next day. If DSI is 25% or under, watch for an upmove the next several days, most likely the next day.
5. In particular, watch the opening the next day in relation to the closing. We think you'll find some important relationships between extremes on the DSI and the next several days of activity.
6. Watch for several days of extreme readings in relation to significant tops or bottoms.
7. Develop your own method of application.

Constructing Your Own Daily Sentiment Index

Constructing your own market sentiment index is not difficult. Here are some ideas and suggestions:

1. Enlist the cooperation of from fifteen to twenty-five investors, friends, associates, and brokers.

2. Call them daily after market closings and ask whether they are bullish or bearish on the market.

3. Record a bullish response as a plus sign next to the name of the respondent and a bearish response as a minus sign. (I count a neutral response as a bearish response since neutrality suggests apathy or an unwillingness to participate in the market.)

4. Tally up the results and arrive at a percentage bullish figure.

5. Share the results with your group as their reward for participating in the daily survey.

6. Plot the percentage bullish response daily against closing stock prices from the Dow Jones industrial averages or Standard & Poor's 500.

Use the interpretive guidelines provided in this book as your guide for evaluating and acting on high or low daily sentiment index numbers. As an alternative to conducting your own survey, you can contact my offices for information on how to obtain our readings daily.

The public is not always wrong. There have been and will be times during which public sentiment prevails. Market sentiment must be very bullish or very bearish, however, and it must come in response to market events. A very high bullish sentiment reading when prices are trending sideways or when no significant cyclical turn is due is not necessarily to be taken as a reliable indication of change.

Remember also that sentiment can change rapidly. Although 90 percent of traders can be bearish on the market for several days, their opinions can change rapidly as prices turn higher and the public becomes bullish. Such quick changes are useful to the short-term cyclically oriented trader, but they are not necessarily meaningful to long-term investors, who are advised to monitor such indices as OLSS and put/call ratios during the time window of anticipated market turns for more precise timing.

Chapter 16

Investor Psychology, Stocks, and Cycles

The preceding chapters describe numerous technical indicators, theories, and methods designed to help you analyze, find, time, buy, and sell stocks based on repetitive price patterns. These techniques are not perfect. They result in losing stock selections if strict discipline and risk management rules are not followed. As simple as this may sound in theory, it is difficult to put in practice. Once the charts have been analyzed, the indicators have been studied, and the conclusions have been reached, the decisions must be put into action. For many investors, however, the leap from decision to action, from realization to actualization, is a dangerous one. Sadly, many investors are unable to put decisions into action, and when action is taken it often is not carried through to the conclusion that is determined by investment methodology.

The weakest element of investment success is not the investor's system or method but the individual who is responsible for decision making. There are many good methods for selecting stocks, and most of them are simple to understand and apply, but the investor ultimately translates the facts into action by taking the appropriate steps at the prescribed times and by acting consistently, confidently, and with persistence. I cannot overemphasize the importance of understanding why investors fail and of knowing oneself. Both are essential to the formula for lasting investment success in stocks, futures, real estate, or other areas of business. The professional investor, like the professional athlete, requires discipline and practice.

How Investors Go Wrong

Emotion is the enemy of speculators and investors, and market highs and lows are characterized by intense emotion. At tops the burning need to buy is virtually all that investors can feel. Those who have not been aboard the bull move throw caution to the wind and jump into the market, buying virtually any stock for virtually any reason—real, rumored, or imagined. The feeling that prompts such behavior is not greed but a feeling that is carried from childhood—the fear that one will be left out or forgotten, that other children will get a piece of candy but this one won't. Investors who watch as the market or a stock moves higher can intellectualize, rationalize, and make all manner of excuses to explain their lack of action, yet as prices continue higher the realization that they were wrong begins to set in. By now it is most likely too late, but they must act to preserve their self-respect. For a variety of reasons, they may have rejected forty opportunities to get into a move, or they may have taken a few opportunities but lacked the discipline to wait for the move and took a loss or perhaps a very small profit for fear the move wouldn't continue. Eventually they reject their fear and jump. Typically, by the time this level of frustration and self-flagellation have been reached, the market is near its peak. It has had to literally slap the investor in the face with its unbridled strength to arouse action. It therefore is not greed that gets an investor to buy at or near the top of a move.

Greed, however, is alive and well. It resides in the heart of those who are already on the correct side of the market. As their investments grow, so does their optimism, which eventually gives way to a feeling of omnipotence, which eventually leads to greed. Once investors begin to feel that they can do no wrong, a type of tunnel vision makes them hold on too long, ignoring the obvious signs of a change in trend and adding to a position, averaging their cost up.

But let's not forget about the evils of fear. Fear of loss causes investors to avoid stocks. Although many investors hesitate to buy stocks for fear of taking a loss, still others are afraid to liquidate a losing position for fear of having to admit to the loss. But fear is greatest when the investor decides whether to sell short. After all, to sell a stock short means facing virtually unlimited risk since there is no limit to how high a stock can go. To buy is a far safer proposition because the most you can lose is all you've invested; and this rarely happens. Investors' fear of losing more than they invested is precisely what keeps the average investor away from the short side of the market, even though markets drop much faster than they rise and sell indicators and signals are often much more reliable, accurate, and profitable than are buy signals.

Other emotions and feelings may stand in the way of success or hasten the road to failure. Of these, lack of confidence, or self-doubt, is among the worst. Although an investor may have access to some of the most potentially valuable and profitable investment advice possible, lack of confidence may result in the advice either not being used or being applied inconsistently or incorrectly. Lack of confidence is usually a behavior that is learned from early experiences and has likely plagued the investor for years and in virtually every area of his or her life. Regardless of its origin, it is, fortunately, simple to recognize and is reasonably responsive to techniques that may change it.

Another factor that causes investors to take unnecessary losses or to miss profitable opportunities is the fear of success. Some people fear success as much as they fear failure. Those who fail can always look forward to success, while those who succeed can only look ahead to the next challenge. In the 1970s I became acquainted with one of the most successful futures traders of all time. He had amassed a fortune in little over a year by following a very simple but very good futures trading system he had developed. Continued success seemed certain. The question was not "Would he continue to be successful?" but "How much money would he make?" Within a year he shocked the financial community by losing all his money back to the market. Several years later I had the opportunity to ask him how he viewed his rise and fall. Following several minutes of reflection he said, "If you're a mountain climber, then your goal is to reach the top of the mountain. And when you get to the top, there's nowhere to go but down." It was not too much later than he again rose to the top only to fall again not long thereafter. Was it fear of success that was his undoing, or was it the need to compete, the need to feel challenged? There are individuals who cannot cope with the pressures of having to outperform their own achievements. Rather than continue to aim for higher and higher goals they slip back, or perhaps they never achieve success for fear of the pressures it might bring.

Finally, consider the plight of the individual who sees investing as a game. Instead of profits, he or she seeks the thrill of the game. Such an attitude is not necessarily inconsistent with success, but it may not bring lasting success. Those who invest or trade in order to merely play the game may be addicted to chance taking or thrill seeking. If you find yourself looking for stocks to buy or trade and altering your rules in order to find something to trade, then you are most likely approaching the business of investing from the wrong perspective.

What Can You Do?

Some simple and effective professional techniques have been used to change unwanted or counterproductive behaviors. There are at least two major schools of thought regarding problem behaviors. According to the psychoanalytical point of view most behavior disorders begin in early childhood and affect adult behavior through unconscious psychological processes. In order to change such behaviors it is necessary to explore the past, perhaps relive it, and certainly understand it in terms of both its actual effects and its symbolic meanings.

The behavioral point of view agrees that although such behaviors may originate in childhood, their cure does not necessarily require many hours of traditional psychoanalysis. The behaviorist maintains that such behaviors are learned and that they may be "unlearned" through the application of specific techniques that are based on the principles of learning. Many methods have proven highly effective. In order to learn more about these you can read one or more of the many books on behavioral learning theory and behavioral therapy or consult a behaviorally oriented therapist in order to effect a course of treatment. Typically such treatment is not as lengthy or expensive an undertaking as are most forms of traditional psychotherapy, and it can have virtually immediate and lasting results.

Those who recognize that they may be limiting their success may benefit from the following recommendations adapted from my book *The Investor's Quotient:* [1]

1. *Plan your trades specifically and in advance.* Keep them available. A concise plan can help you avoid spur-of-the-moment decisions that lead to costly errors.

---

1. Adapted from Bernstein, J., *The Investor's Quotient* (New York: John Wiley & Sons, 1980), 175–178.

2. *Realize that you are responsible for the success of your trading.* Once you learn that you control your profits and losses, you will avoid emotional decisions, cease blaming others for errors, and, most important, act consistently within your trading system.

3. *Avoid hoping that a position will go your way and fearing that a position will not go your way.* Hope and fear lead to unrealistic expectations, emotional decisions, and negative attitudes.

4. *Monitor your performance.* Keep a thorough record of how your system is working to know how well you are doing at any one point in time.

5. *Maintain a positive attitude.* Combat the negative effects of losses, interference from others, and poor trading signals. A positive attitude is an important asset to successful trading.

6. *Cultivate effective and positive relationships.* Seek out individuals who are highly motivated to achieve, have ambitious goals, and are willing to work to overcome obstacles. They can teach you positive skills and attitudes.

7. *Don't take home the market.* The market is a means to an end and not a way of life. Don't let it interfere with other areas of your life. Take time each year to close out positions and take vacations.

8. *Enjoy the fruits of your labor.* Remove profits from the market regularly, perhaps monthly. Spending and saving profits help motivate.

9. *Avoid overconfidence and underconfidence.* Being at either emotional extreme can impair your judgment. The best course is to even out the peaks and valleys. Overconfidence, in fact, can lead you to take chances that can destroy you.

10. *Keep your next goal in sight.* Once you have attained an objective, set your next challenge. If you have another mountain to climb, you won't be tempted to return to the bottom in order to confront a new challenge.

Chapter 17

How Stock Cycles Can Work for You

Despite my efforts to quantify and operationalize the systems, methods, and procedures involved in the process of cyclic analysis, the use of cycles in stock trading remains an art as well as a science. Today, eight years after publication of *The Handbook of Commodity Cycles: A Window on Time,*[1] considerably more is known about technical and timing indicators that facilitate the cyclic method, yet cyclic techniques are still subject to interpretation.

Few professionals in the field can be consulted for verification. In one sense this is good because it shows that most investors are not looking at cycles, and since the majority is usually wrong, some degree of comfort can be taken in being part of the minority. On the other hand, the relative lack of professional practitioners leaves the cycles trader in a lonely place. The Foundation for the Study of Cycles is an excellent organization providing quality research, but it is not staffed with investment advisers. A few advisory publications claim to analyze cycles. Some brokers claim to use cycles in their trading and research, but their potential conflict of interest and their heavy client load makes it difficult for nonclients to consult with them.

The cycles trader persists with a nagging insecurity that he or she is out there alone. Though an element of excitement accompanies this lonely voyage, it is not the kind of excitement that serious investors seek. Traders want answers and direction.

The problem also arises as to how one might obtain, implement,

---

1. *The Handbook of Commodity Cycles: A Window on Time* (New York: John Wiley & Sons, 1982).

analyze, and execute the kind of information and systematization that are likely to produce profitable results. I certainly don't have all the answers, and many of the answers I do have are subject to additional verification, validation, and alternation. My work in the field of cycles has evolved since 1972, but it is relatively minor compared to the work that still needs to be done. However, I know that the individual trader or investor can put cycles to work in a trading program of either short-term, intermediate-term, or long-term duration. This chapter provides some concrete guidelines to keep you on track and mindful of your goals.

Decide on Your Time Orientation

Time frame is the single most important decision an investor must make. Although the desire to work in all time frames (short-term, intermediate-term, long-term) is natural, very few individuals can achieve this objective consistently. Working in all three time frames is limited not only by the amount of time available but also by the psychological effect of time-frame interaction. Investors frequently have difficulty establishing a position based in one time frame and then establishing an opposite position using a different time frame. The tendency is to confuse time frames and use signals from one time frame in another.

For the new investor or for one who is becoming reacquainted with the marketplace, I recommend finding one time frame that makes you comfortable and staying with it as your major time orientation. Only after you have gained considerable experience with your chosen time frame should you consider adding or switching. Whatever you decide, make sure that you *do* decide. You may wish to study or analyze all three time frames, but invest using only one of these initially.

Determine Your Risk Capital

Knowing your risk is an important aspect of investing. Investors can and do lose money, and losers probably outnumber winners. Nothing is definite when it comes to profit. But the individual who starts with a larger amount of risk capital is more likely to succeed than is the individual who has little to risk. The individual who can risk more is probably a more sophisticated, more knowledgeable, and wealthier individual and probably is not as prone to run scared before his or her system indicates that taking a loss is appropriate. Finally, most systems take time to test.

Consider these facts when making your decision about how much risk you are willing to accept. The less you can afford, the less likely are your chances of success, regardless of the trading system you plan to employ. Furthermore, you must have the discipline to stay with your original intentions. If you have decided you can risk $10,000 and you lose it all, don't add more unless you have more risk capital available.

Be Organized

Organization is third on my list of prerequisites. Investors frequently lose money for reasons other than the inherent inaccuracies or randomness of their stock selection system. Such errors are avoidable through the use of consistent, organized, and disciplined trading rules. Since the odds of profitable trading for many trading systems are between 60 and 75 percent, don't decrease these already low odds by committing unnecessary blunders that are not related to the system itself. Perhaps the best way to keep the odds in your favor is to eliminate most, if not all, nonsystem errors. This can be accomplished by a logical, organized approach.

Stock Selection Methodology is Not
First on the List

The approach or methodology used in selecting stocks is not first on my list because I don't regard it as the single most important aspect of investing. Cyclic and seasonal analysis are certainly both valid and worthwhile techniques, but they are very broad methods. They need to be narrowed down to make them specific and pragmatic. Unless you make investing your full-time occupation, you won't be able to study all of the relevant indicators. For example, you may decide that seasonal analysis and seasonal trends are the most logical in terms of your personal situation. If short-term cyclic analysis is best suited for you, then determine how you will implement short-term techniques. These are all important considerations relating to techniques.

Evaluate and work with some of the indicators presented, so you will feel at home with them. Retain the ones that work best for you. Once you have formulated all these concepts, considered all the facts that require deliberation and development, and made the necessary decisions, you're ready to trade.

Observe and Record

Many investors are more perceptive than I am. When they begin to work with cycles, markets, and indicators, they may observe relationships and parameters that I have not found. I hope that this book will stimulate you to do additional research to develop new indicators that will serve you better. If you are observant and keep records of your trades and signals, you will learn from the many nuances that take years of experience to acquire. Each exposure to the market, each analytical session, and each of your studies should be a learning experience to verify that something works, that something is going on, that something doesn't work, or that nothing is going on. These are vital and significant pieces of information for the investor. Observe them and learn!

Money Management

Effective money management is critical to the success of any investment program. The way your account is managed may be the determining factor in success or failure. Regardless of your system of stock selection, it is of secondary importance if it is not instituted within the guidelines of sensible and effective money management. There are three fundamental elements of good money management:

1. Do not overextend your margin. A good rule of thumb is to have no more than 50 percent of available capital committed to the market at any point in time.

2. Don't ride losses. In other words, don't let a small loss turn into a large one. Take those losses when your system says to do so—no sooner, no later.

3. Avoid markets that would require you to take too much risk relevant to your account size.

Before you begin trading with the cycles approach—or, for that matter, any system or method—be prepared: Know your methods and procedures and study your alternatives and game plan. Develop sufficient confidence to avoid unnecessary errors. Not many individuals can stick with the guidelines of a totally mechanical system. In the long run, those individuals who can develop and maintain a trading system that is, perhaps, 75 percent automatic probably will fare very well. Note that I do not advise a 100 percent mechanical or automatic approach to cycles. Since cycles and the cyclic approach are not 100 percent reliable, the investor must employ some degree of judgment.

The importance of research cannot be overemphasized. To thoroughly test and evaluate all of the indicators presented in this book would take considerable effort and funds. The complexity of testing all indicators in conjunction with one another at cyclic turns adds yet another dimension of cost and effort. My work—though tested thoroughly for a limited time sample in some cases and a more lengthy time sample in other cases—is by no means complete. In fact, by the time this book is in print the characteristics of many markets may have changed sufficiently to alter the efficacy of certain indicators. This is why I urge you to do your own research, even if it is limited to manual methods as opposed to computerized study.

Chapter 18

Quintessential Issues in Cyclic Analysis

Due to the changeable nature of markets, a totally mechanical system probably never will prove to be a consistent performer over time. Trend-following methods such as moving-average systems perform as a function of trend. Systems based on cyclic trend following work best when trends are relatively free of whipsaw behavior.

My approach to cyclic analysis is not mechanical; it's clear to me that cycles are at least partially subjective. Ultimately, each individual must think and act based on a good understanding of the marketplace.

Investing can be facilitated by forms of artificial intelligence, especially those that allow users to learn from their experiences. Yet a functional balance is needed between the rationality, speed, objectivity of the computer and the creativity of the human mind. The single most important aspect of cyclic analysis—or for that matter, of any trading approach—is an understanding of how the approach functions within the context of the marketplace. This chapter examines that issue from the theoretical and pragmatic perspectives essential to the proper implementation of cyclic techniques.

The Importance of Understanding Price, Time, and Cycle Relationships

Price cycles are relatively independent from human reactions to events and factors prompted by human actions. Cyclic patterns have certainly been distorted by war, and yet various researchers have demonstrated that cyclic tendencies occur even in times of international conflict; to a certain extent, in fact, such conflict can be predicted using cycles. Seasonal patterns are only partially determined by humankind and are a function of various economic forces as well as weather patterns. Cycles, therefore, are naturally imposed time spans that maintain validity through their repetitions. Understanding cycles can add immeasurably to an effective ongoing analysis of supply and demand because price cycles are a backdrop against which price relationships are measured by the supply-and-demand equation. Ultimately, price cycles probably have their basis in patterns of human consumption that may be prompted or regulated by astronomical or geophysical events such as magnetic fields, polar ice-cap shifts, planetary alignment, sunspots, as well as many other unknown forces. Nevertheless, achieving an effective understanding of virtually any market situation is possible by a concise analysis of price, time, cycles, and the relationship between buyers and sellers. Price and time interact to create opportunity.

Basic Unit of Analysis

Virtually all decisions are facilitated when cycles are used as the basic unit of market analysis. Determining when price cycles have reached their top or bottom is facilitated by examining the time window (or ideal time frame for a turn) and timing (the response of buyers and sellers).

Price is a method by which buyers and sellers are attracted to a market. Ultimately, price must go high enough to attract all significant sellers or low enough to draw in all significant buyers. Therefore, the function of price is, as Peter Steidlmayer[1] suggests, to advertise for market participants. Both the status of the cycle and the activity of buyers and sellers as measured by timing indicators are important elements of cyclic methods. Cycles can be progressing, topping, or bottoming. Buyers and sellers can either respond or wait.

---

1. Steidlmayer, J. Peter and Kevin Koy. *Markets and Market Logic.* (Chicago: Porcupine Press, 1986).

What Makes Cycles Late or Early?

The interaction of price, time (cycles), and market response accounts for early cycle tops or bottoms or late cycle tops or bottoms. In a cycle down, an early bottom is indicated by buyers' willingness to step into a market or an absence of sellers prior to the ideal low. A late cycle bottom is probable when buyers are unwilling to act at current prices or when sellers are still willing to pursue their course of action.

The task of the cyclic analyst is to determine when sellers are in control, when buyers are in control, and when the balance is shifting or has indeed shifted. When this balance shifts during the proper time frame of a probable cycle turn, investor risk will be at its minimum and potential reward will be at its maximum. Timing indicators are designed to detect such balance shifts. Yet you don't need to be one of those brave souls who seeks to participate only in areas of major turn. Because price cycles tend to progress in a stepwise fashion, sufficient time usually exists to evaluate a change in trend (that is, in the buyer/ seller balance) and to act consistently with the new cyclic trend or to take advantage of price reactions within the new trend. You need not buy only at the extreme low or sell at the extreme high in order to be successful.

Fundamental Considerations in Cyclic Analysis

The technical trader often is said to have little or no use for fundamentals. In fact, many traders claim that fundamentals become known only after the fact and that technical considerations tend to forecast fundamental changes in the supply-and-demand situation of markets. Other technical traders maintain that a knowledge of fundamentals is counterproductive to their goals and objectives because it frequently prompts them to take actions inconsistent with their technical indicators. Yet others claim that only insiders are aware of important fundamentals at the right time. I have been guilty at times of underplaying the role of fundamentals and the importance of fundamental changes and developments. For the purely technical trader who follows a totally mechanical or artificial intelligence approach to the marketplace, fundamentals may indeed be a minor consideration. I have learned that fundamentals are useful to all traders in various ways. The following discussion reviews fundamentals as they relate to cycle trading and provides a number of situations and applications of fundamentals that could prove profitable for those who incorporate cyclic analysis in their trading approach.

Traditionally, fundamentals consist of the basic economic factors that are purported to play an important role in the supply-and-demand and price structure of the marketplace. These factors may have either a short-term or long-term effect on prices, or they may play a secondary role. Such things as supply-and-demand statistics, foreign orders, exchange rates, foreign competitive products, gross national product, inventories, and a host of other statistics are often considered part of the fundamental structure of stocks. Some fundamentals are relatively intangible; others appear to have a direct effect on prices. As a rule, any one or several fundamentals may affect price-trend developments for a relatively brief time, but some fundamentals, such as an abrupt change in weather patterns or other natural catastrophes, can have a severe and lasting effect on prices. It ordinarily is not possible for fundamental forces to make a major shift without markedly affecting prices. Large institutional traders have good contact with fundamentals throughout the world and take action in anticipation of changes based on these factors, and monitoring their activity can help determine the development of the next major move. Because they are aware that their activities may be closely monitored by others, they can take measures to mask their entry into and exit from the marketplace.

Contrary Nature of the Market

Investors are aware that fundamentals are frequently known in advance by professionals and that prices often fail to respond to the current fundamentals. Instead, they tend to show their greatest response when the fundamentals are about to change in another direction. Fundamentals and market direction often seem out of phase. For example, consider situations in which fundamental factors are at their most bullish very close to the top of the market and most bearish toward the bottom of the market. Those dedicated to the fundamental approach will argue that this situation is illusory and that the important fundamentals are not known or traders are not aware of their developing importance. Those dedicated to technical analysis will correctly argue that fundamentals are reflected in prices and that since prices are an effect of fundamentals, studying price trends and relationships will help investors ascertain the existing and anticipated trends of the marketplace. As in many cases of polarized thought, the truth is likely to be found somewhere in the middle. Technical and fundamental considerations are both important and both can provide valuable data. Both types of information create opportunities for traders, and these opportunities can facilitate profitable trading, particularly at major market turning points. The main consideration is that fundamentals and technicals must be taken within the context of the cyclic patterns. Market response to fundamentals and technicals is more important than the timing signals generated by fundamental or technical factors.

Evaluating Market Response

Numerous factors influence the action of buyers and sellers in the marketplace and shape investor or trader attitudes and expectations. Two individuals examining the same set of statistics can arrive at two opposite conclusions due to expectation, anticipation, attitude, and perception. This is where the marketplace fulfills its function. It provides buyers and sellers with an avenue of expression called buying and selling.

The quintessential aspect of market information is buyer and seller response. A trader or investor who holds an opinion or who does not translate the effect of a news item into action is not a significant force in the marketplace. There are three basic potential market responses to fundamental or technical issues:

1. No response,
2. Consistent response (that is, buying in response to bullish news and selling in response to bearish news), and
3. Opposite response (that is, selling in response to bullish news and buying in response to bearish news).

A generally accepted maxim in the marketplace is that traders should buy on anticipation and sell on realization. In other words, many practice "buy the rumor, sell the news." This is not unreasonable when you remember that the marketplace is an anticipatory game. Traders often buy stocks or futures in anticipation of an up trend or sell in anticipation of a down trend. Knowledgeable traders take advantage of news-created opportunities to establish their positions on the opposite side. For example, bearish news is frequently used to mask entry into long positions by large commercials and knowledgeable speculators. Conversely, bullish news is used as a vehicle for entering large short positions or for liquidating large long positions with relative ease.

Legendary speculator Jesse Livermore once quipped, "It's amazing how much stock there is for sale in a rising market."[2] Fundamental and technical factors cannot be considered bullish or bearish without reference to their effect on the marketplace. A bear market that is barraged almost daily with negative fundamentals and technical considerations but that fails to move lower in response to these factors clearly indicates that bearish news is being used by long-term traders and commercial interests to accumulate significant long positions for a probable up move. Conversely, fundamental and technical developments that should have a bullish effect on prices but consistently fail to do so cannot be considered positive developments. To take a piece of fundamental information out of context is as absurd as evaluating any measurement out of context. It is as absurd as the weather forecaster who jokingly says, "And here are some temperatures from around the country: 63, 72, and a whopping 88 degrees!" This type of information needs a reference point. A whopping 88 degrees in Anchorage, Alaska, for example, would be significant, but in Key West, Florida, the news would be nothing out of the ordinary.

The student of fundamental and technical developments in the marketplace must constantly evaluate all fundamentals for their market effect. Their effect may be immediate or delayed, consistent with past experience or inconsistent with it. In any event, information, whether fundamental or technical, is important only in relation to its effect on the marketplace. Did the information result in an upturn or a down-

---

2. Edwin Le Fevbre [Jesse Livermore]. *Reminiscences of a Stock Operator* (Larchmont, NY: American Research Council, 1965).

turn? Did the information initially result in a downturn followed by an upturn or vice versa? Did the information fail to affect the marketplace? How long did the news take to affect the marketplace? These questions must be asked and their answers analyzed.

How an Investor Can Use This Information

Knowing that a market is due to make a major or minor top or bottom based on the cycles, the investor can begin to evaluate the effect of news on the marketplace. Of course, many other technical indicators could be evaluated in determining the approximate timing of a nine-year cycle low (or any other cycle low or high). Typically at such a bottom, the fundamental considerations will be bearish. Yet the observant investor knows that at some point bearish news will have increasingly less negative effect on the marketplace and may, in fact, have a slowly but surely developing positive effect on prices.

Important fundamental reports initially affect daily trading in a negative fashion, only to be followed later in the day by a reversal of the downturn or a strongly positive response. The bearish fundamentals begin to result in sideways to higher prices, while fundamentals continue to barrage the marketplace with purportedly negative news. In such a situation, the cycles trader can have great confidence in his or her work because the market's response to news clearly demonstrates that the cycle is about to turn higher. Frequently, such responses develop prior to the occurrence of any timing signals. These developments, although difficult to quantify and often subtle, are of great importance.

On occasion, there is a clear demonstration of the market's unwillingness to accept the supposedly negative news in a negative fashion. Such situations are easily detected by traders who know what to watch for. Typically there is an initial negative market response to bearish news, such as a lower daily price opening. The day may end, however, with a higher closing price. The reverse holds true as a cycle is peaking. When presented with a succession of such responses over an extended period of time during the appropriate cyclic time frame, little doubt exists (or ought to exist) in the mind of the cycles trader that an important turn is developing. The market has rejected the news, and lower prices have not been accepted. Consequently, the market has only two choices—to turn sideways or to go higher. The process of rejecting bearish news with bullish market response is a classic situation in a developing cyclic low.

The opposite occurs as a cycle tops: markets are bullish. Bullish news occurs almost day after day; investors, the public, and the press are bullish; and yet the market consistently fails to respond higher on bullish news, indicating to knowledgeable traders that something is definitely wrong. Should this develop in the time frame of a cyclic top, the informed trader has good reason to believe that the top has either developed or is about to occur.

For all these reasons, cycles traders need to understand fundamentals. By knowing market response, lack of response, or opposite response to fundamentals, you have more evidence on which to evaluate cyclic patterns. In addition to the information provided by fundamentals about prices and cycles, fundamental developments and reports can provide you with an opportunity to enter a given market on a trend reaction. To the cycles trader, bearish news in a bullish market constitutes a buying opportunity and vice versa for bullish news in a bear market. News may be your greatest ally. You can take advantage of opportunities created by news to establish positions on reactions within the major trend. Furthermore, the news can be used to liquidate positions within existing trends. Assume that you are holding a short position in a bearish cycle that is approaching the projected end of its move. Assume also that a major bit of fundamental news pushes prices sharply lower on a given day. The well-rounded investor uses such a market reaction as an opportunity to leave the short side because the end of the move is likely to be close at hand. The investor, in this way, can take advantage of fundamental developments in the marketplace that create trading opportunities.

As is apparent, the important factors in evaluating fundamentals are different for the cycles trader than they are for the traditional fundamentalist. Yet these same factors should be important to the fundamentalist, who also is concerned with market response to news and fundamentals. To review my suggestions:

1. Fundamentals are important only to the extent that they affect prices in either the expected or the unexpected direction.

2. Fundamentals are important only to the degree that they prompt speculators or investors to act.

3. Persistent market response to fundamentals in the direction opposite of expectations strongly suggests that the market trend is changing. When this occurs during the time frame of an expected cyclic trend, it is even more significant and constitutes evidence that a trend change either has occurred or is about to occur.

4. Fundamental developments create opportunities for cyclically oriented investors to evaluate, enter, or exit positions.

5. Cycles investors should study market response to fundamental and technical developments to determine the efficacy of these suggestions.

About Risk and Reward

To a great extent, the issue of market response is closely related to the risk and reward aspects of futures trading. Traditional understanding measures risk in terms of dollars or prices, but a different avenue of assessing risk is recommended for the cycles trader. I recommend that risk be evaluated as a function of market behavior. Because cycles and cyclic analysis are not perfect or mechanical, your understanding of conditions in a given market at any point in time will be different from your market understanding at another point in time. In some cases, you will have very little doubt about expected price trends, your analysis of the cycles will be complete, and you will have virtually no uncertainty as to what position you should establish or the direction in which prices are likely to move. In such cases, your risk in trading is relatively small compared to the risk you would take in cases where your understanding of the factors and market interrelationships is unclear. I recommend that you constantly evaluate risk in terms of knowledge as well as technical factors in the marketplace. When your understanding is lowest, your risk is likely to be highest. You will be in doubt about where or when you should buy or sell, as well as where or when you should leave your position, either with a profit or a loss. At times, even a thorough understanding proves to be incorrect, but it can still let you know when you are wrong and when to leave and/or reverse your position.

Should You Do Your Own Work or Should You Use an Advisory Service?

I'm a strong proponent of doing your own work in the marketplace, even if it means that you follow fewer markets. Although many services can be purchased to provide you with some of the charts and information needed to evaluate cyclic patterns, the information you acquire by doing the work yourself is much more valuable because you learn from it. Until you have learned the proper approach and implementation of the trading plan, you should do your own work; you then will have a basis on which to evaluate the work of others and choose a service.

Another point to consider is that few services today provide cycles research consistent with my approach. Many chart services provide the basic information you need, yet the available services that cover cyclic analysis vary significantly in their analytical approaches. This could prove to be confusing. When all is said and done, you will be much better off doing your own analysis as well as your own charting.

Chapter 19

Frequently Asked Questions

Throughout the years I have found that people generally have difficulty with the same issues or topics. This chapter presents some of the questions people frequently ask me along with my answers. I hope that some of your queries will be addressed and resolved; if not, I invite you to write me.

Q. What is a good charting service?

A. There are many excellent charting services that the cyclic investor can use. Before choosing, obtain a sample of each service and make sure that the one you ultimately select contains the following features:

1. Charts should be large, preferable 8½ × 11 inches or larger.
2. Charts should be designed to permit easy and regular user updating.
3. Each chart should have enough blank space to the right to permit the projection of the next one or two cycles.
4. Weekly and monthly charts should be provided on a regular basis. The service should not analyze the markets, nor should it make recommendations or provide other information.
5. Logscale charts and charts cluttered with earnings information should be avoided.

Many computer quote systems allow you to view daily, weekly, monthly, and intraday charts as well. Some of these computer quote systems permit the overlay of many of the studies described in this book. In view of the many alternatives, I recommend that you take the time to sample various services before selecting what suits you best. I will gladly advise you of my preferences if you drop me a line.

Q. Why not include all calendar days when counting cycles?

A. When counting daily cycle lengths I include only days on which a market is open, but this is not the only valid way to count cycles. Using market days or calendar days results in an approximate time frame during which prices are likely to change direction. Whatever approach you employ, however, you should do so consistently.

Q. Should my stop loss orders be "in the market"?

A. Some investors claim that stop losses or other resting orders have a tendency to be "picked off" by specialists. They also feel that this occurs only to their disadvantage. In other words, if they are long a market, with stop loss below the market, they fear that the market will come down to hit their stop. This is one of the most popular suspicions about resting orders. Consequently, many investors prefer not to enter their orders but rather to act at a given price or at the market when necessary. I don't see any particular problem with this procedure, yet I don't subscribe entirely to the school of thought that promotes the stop-picking argument.

You have three choices regarding the implementation of stop losses or buy/sell stops: first, you can enter a stop with your broker; second, you can have a stop; third, which usually is not given much consideration in most trading systems, you can use no stops during the trading day but rather use closing prices or opening prices to generate signals. Such an approach has not been given sufficient consideration because it fails to conform to many of the principles of sound money management. Given sufficient thought and consideration, this sensible approach could be developed into operational procedures.

If a position in the market is the "right" position, then the use of buy or sell stops consistent with or as required by the system should not be a cause for concern. Some markets are notorious for "picking off" resting stops, but the serious cycles investor should not be overly concerned since the cyclic methods employed should keep him or her on the right track. Stops, their use, and precise manner of execution are specifically related to the trader's needs and modus operandi. There may be some validity to the fear that resting orders will be triggered, but this is true only in thinly traded markets and for very large positions.

Q.   How do news, government reports, and inside information affect the cycles?

A.   This is one of the most commonly asked questions and probably the simplest to answer. My experience with cycles strongly suggests that cycles anticipate most of these events and that these occurrences rarely develop out of phase with the cycles. Though cycles are not perfect, they do seem to have an uncanny ability to forecast major market events.

News often provides an entry opportunity within a given cyclic time frame. A bearish report released during a strong cyclic bull market will probably result in a price reaction or decline into a support area, followed by a move to higher price levels. Though I would certainly say that the news should be ignored most of the time, acting contrary to the news is often a very sensible policy, particularly when there are good cyclic reasons for trading from a given market orientation.

Q.   Why aren't cycles more accurate?

A.   If we could know all the different cyclic periods operating in conjunction at any given point in time, we probably could formulate a very accurate synthesis of all the cycles and project tops and bottoms (as well as prices) more accurately. However, since not all the inputs are knowns, turns cannot be predicted as accurately as we might like. If cycles were perfect, markets, theories of cycles, and timing indicators would not be needed. Nature, itself, which is probably the cause of cycles, is not perfect, but cycles are much more accurate than we know. Our inability to completely understand the machinery of cyclic cause and effect, however, limits our ability to make more accurate determinations of tops and bottoms. Advanced computer methods and hardware technology will undoubtedly lead to greater accuracy in the years to come.

Q.   How much profit can I expect to make trading with the cyclic approach?

A.   That depends on you. There are so many variables in the study and implementation of cycles that I would certainly be out of line if I gave you a specific answer. Two traders can use the same basic tools, but one can win and the other lose. I have no specific guidelines, nor can I claim that a clear understanding of cyclic trading will make you money. The application of cycles—or, for that matter, any trading system—is an individual matter. There is a certain amount of art to the science of cyclical investing.

Q. Is it possible to predict prices using cycles?

A. Using cycles to predict or project prices is not a scientific procedure. Although I have illustrated some techniques that can be employed to this end, I generally do not favor using cycles for price prediction because cycles are time-based indicators. Price itself is relatively unimportant and can be at any level when cycles turn. I suggest that you pay less attention to price and more attention to cycles and timing indicators. Looking merely at price probably will dissuade you from making trades as a function of price levels because most of us have been conditioned to think in terms of price, price level, historical price level, and value. The concepts of value, relative value, historical highs and lows, and recent price history are certainly valid tools as an adjunct to cyclic investing, but price alone should not be used for trade selection. Some trading systems and methods employ price derivations extensively in their analyses, but as part of my cyclic approach, they play only a secondary role in terms of timing.

Q. What is the best way to get started trading with cycles?

A. You should have a thorough understanding of the principles, philosophy, and indicators discussed in this book. An understanding of the basics of futures trading is certainly a prerequisite. Once you have mastered these, once you know your direction, the best way to get started is simply to begin. There is no better teacher than hands-on experience. I recommend only a minimal period of paper trading prior to hands-on or real-time experience in the markets. Take the plunge, make some stock investments, keep your positions small, your risk relatively low, and your objectives reasonable. Experience is the best teacher.

Q. Can you refer me to a good broker?

A. It has been my experience that one investor's good broker is not necessarily a good broker to another. I prefer minimal broker input and maximum broker service and have no need for brokerage house research, reports, recommendations, etc. Why pay for it? Investors often can be swayed from their own valid opinions by input from brokers and other sources. If you cannot filter the input of brokers, knowing what to accept and what to reject, then I suggest you secure the services of a discount brokerage firm, one that provides prompt and efficient order execution, reasonably low commissions, and courteous service. I have my personal preferences about brokers, but the decision must ultimately be yours. Do your homework and find the firm or firms that you can work with best. Remember that price alone must not be the final factor on which your decision is made.

Chapter 20

Computer Technology and
Its Role in Cyclic Analysis
and Investing

In the early 1980s computer technology made enormous advances. Computers that once needed to be the size of several large refrigerators can process the same amount of information in a space the size of a small typewriter. The information that once needed to be stored on large disks now can be stored on small diskettes. Prices have moved down. Having access to powerful technology for a reasonable price has been a great boon to technical traders and investors. The chart studies and analyses that once took many tedious hours to complete now can be performed by computers in a matter of minutes or seconds and with greater accuracy.

New software performs highly complex mathematical manipulations of raw data that were previously either impossible or too costly to perform. In addition to the hardware and software revolutions, stock data have become dramatically more available. Many years of historical data can be obtained at a reasonable price, as can tick-by-tick data for the purpose of studying intraday and short-term patterns. Serious investors, whether short term, long term, or even intermediate term, need a computer system and access to either on-line or stored historical data. Any discussion of which computer systems are best suited for stock analysis would be obsolete by the time this book reaches you. Excellent product reviews are available that cover hardware and software for futures traders and investors. This chapter simply provides some general guidelines for evaluating any computer system, present or future.

Prepackaged or Original?

In selecting a computer system that will help analyze stock prices, investors can either buy a prepackaged system one that is specifically designed for the analysis of stock data or create an individualized system. One advantage of the prepackaged system is that everything you need to do has already been done for you. The systems have self-contained data-analysis software to provide the studies you may wish to perform and quotations systems that provide prices needed for ongoing market analyses. Many systems have graphics that display charts on a screen and can be transferred to paper (hard copy) by a printer or plotter. Such systems seem to be ideally suited to the stock investor because they can provide the information you think you need, but they do not allow you to move beyond the capabilities of the software package. The ideal computer system will permit investors to identify specific variables and systems that they want to test in conjunction with the data. This flexibility is required for effective research and development.

Another drawback to buying a prepackaged system is that other individuals who acquire the same system will analyze the data and act on many of the same signals and indicators in virtually the same way as you will. This could prove to be detrimental to your performance, since the market may be affected by many traders entering and exiting markets at the same time. Although most prepackaged systems offer the necessary basic features, they may not provide features needed to do original research on stock prices and cycles.

One type of prepackaged computer system that lends itself readily to commodity analysis works on the user's-group principle. The user buys a computer system that is compatible with the particular data and services offered by a given organization and then subscribes to the service, paying a monthly fee (or membership fee). The group frequently uses different technical approaches and trading programs, many of which deal with the statistical analyses relating to cyclic studies. Frequent access to these programs is available at a standard charge.

Assuming that you have your own prepackaged system or one served by a user's group, you have no need to read any further because most of the decisions about memory, storage, graphics, printer, and service already have been made for you. I encourage individuals to strike out on their own, however, searching for original techniques, employing their own programs, and doing their own research. This type of approach often produces unique results.

Memory

In the early days of computer technology memory was an important feature, and most computer research centered on the development of systems that provided more memory. During the 1980s, however, advanced technology made available extremely large amounts of memory at exceptionally low prices. In the old days, 32 kilobytes of memory was standard, and 256 kilobytes considered large; today several megabytes of memory is not uncommon. A large memory is certainly desirable because it lets the user employ complex programming, which allows faster information processing and less user interaction. Complex mathematical procedures that require great amounts of memory and intermediate storage in memory today can be achieved with more efficiency and greater speed. But most analytical work does not need memory larger than 1 megabyte. Every dollar spent does not necessarily produce another dollar in terms of results. I recommend purchasing a system with expandable memory capability that will be able to handle efficiently and with reasonable speed the work you need to accomplish. Spend your extra money on good graphics, fast printing, and larger disk storage.

Storage

One of the weakest links in a computer system is storage capability—the amount of information that can be stored in the computer without being placed in active memory. The storage capability of the computer is, in many ways, like a telephone book that the computer accesses when it needs certain programs or data. The more storage you have at your disposal, the more data you can keep in the machine at any time without having to change disks. As you accumulate more data for analysis, your need for high-capacity storage increases. A key consideration in purchasing a computer system is the amount of storage the system has or the amount of storage that can be added to the system. Based on current technology, 40 megabytes of storage is reasonable. Storage is just as important as memory size.

Graphics

Another feature to consider when buying a computer system is its ability to display high-resolution graphics. You want to see, in chart form on your screen, the results of the particular system or cyclic method you are testing. This avoids the time and expense of plotting or printing the data to paper. Contemporary trends are toward color-graphics monitors; although certainly an interesting feature, color graphics are not a necessity.

Printer

An equally important consideration is the printer, which can be the slowest link in the chain. A slow printer can interrupt your entire operation while the computer waits for the printer to finish its work. A fast printer is desirable; alternatively, a printer buffer or spooler can be helpful. For chart printing I strongly recommend a laser printer.

Service

Most service problems should be resolved within twenty-four hours. Active futures traders with considerable funds in the market should consider a standby system for those rare occasions when their hardware fails. Down time costs money and can result in losses or smaller profits. Remember also that minor brand hardware may not be as readily serviced as are the major brands.

Software

You need software compatible with your stock system and methods of analysis. Though you may want to develop your own software, data suppliers generally market data transmission software in formats compatible with popular hardware systems. Though fewer and fewer choices are available as the hardware giants win out over their competitors, many hardware clone systems sell at lower prices than the popular brands. They run major brands of software just as well as the well-known brands of hardware, so shop around and save money.

Chapter 21

Finding Your Way

Because most systems and methods are used (and abused) by people, investors must consider their assets, liabilities, abilities, and capabilities with regard to any system or technique. With so many different cycles, seasonals, patterns, and methods, determining where you fit into the cyclic picture is a difficult task. If, for example, you decide to be an investor, you will use techniques, methods, and systems consistent with your selection. If you decide that you are best at short-term trading, you will examine data, charts, patterns, methods, and techniques consistent with this strategy. Your work will be more focused and more committed to money management and sound trading principles than it would have been had you selected long-term trading. You may decide that you want to use cycles for the purpose of hedging crops or livestock. If this is the case, you will need to study the types of cycles and data that allow you to make the specialized decisions required of you as a producer or end user. In addition, the psychologies of short-term versus long-term trading are distinctly different and must be internalized.

This chapter can help you determine where you belong in the vast world of cyclic trading. Assessing your goals, objectives, abilities, techniques, and motivation will help you determine more precisely your best fit. Once you have found your niche, you can trade with confidence and direction. Consider the following points in making your decision. Honesty is the best policy.

Financial Ability

The most important factor in determining the type of cycle investing that best suits you is your financial ability. Market conditions change from month to month and year to year, so it is difficult to state with finality the amount of capital required for a particular orientation to the market. Generally, however, some comparisons are reasonable considerations when making such a decision. For example, the individual who is willing to trade high-risk positions for short-term moves needs to be more highly capitalized than the individual who tends to trade for long-term moves with reasonably low risk. On the other hand, some individuals who wish to invest for major long-term moves may want to take larger risks using wider stops. In such instances, more capital would be required than in the case of individuals wishing to trade for short-term moves with very small stops.

Short-Term Trading for Limited Risk or with Small Stop Losses

With this approach a relatively small amount of capital is required to trade cycles. Such techniques often result in a fairly long string of losses, however, quickly depleting one's capital. Although it might seem that less risk is taken using such an approach, in the long run more capital may actually be lost since the total number of losses may be large. The smaller your starting capital, the more stringent you'll need to be in your money-management program. Consider, too, that the individual who cannot take a small loss when it should be taken may eventually take a much larger loss than he or she should. What may seem to involve less risk may result in more risk and more losses. Before you decide to become a short-term trader using short-term cycles and short-term techniques, develop a firm approach to money management. Don't let your losses run larger than they should. The most certain way to deplete a small amount of starting capital is to allow your losses to run away from you.

Intermediate-Term Cycles with "Reasonable" Stops

Another approach to cycles trading is based on the use of intermediate-term cycles, such as those discussed in this book. Because cyclic timing can never be as exact as we would wish, wide stops are preferable. Assuming that you commit 5 percent risk on any one position, a fairly large account size is necessary. The concern with this approach is that sufficient capital needs to be available to meet the requirements and to permit several successive losses while keeping the account size large enough to maintain positions. The intermediate-term time frame is adequate for most investors but requires a great deal of patience and discipline, two qualities that are as important as finances.

The Long-Term Approach

If you have discipline of steel and the patience of a saint, the long-term approach is probably the single best application of cycles. Unfortunately, few can employ this approach with discipline and organization. In my many years of trading I have not met more than a handful of individuals who have achieved success in trading for the long term. A discussion of the many reasons for this inability is beyond the scope of this book.[1]

The long-term investor, of course, seeks to capture major moves and is willing to risk taking large losses in order to make large profits. A risk of 10 percent, for example, may eventually yield a 200 percent profit. The difficulty in implementing such an approach is not unwillingness to take the necessary risk but instead the inability of most individuals to be patient while awaiting the opportunity to enter or exit at the optimum time. No matter what your trading system may be, it is useless unless you can administer it effectively. Long-term trading with cycles is rewarding, but it requires large stops, considerable patience, and enormous discipline.

Commitment

The availability of sufficient capital for trading is merely one variable in the success equation. Others are willingness and ability to remain dedicated to a trading system. Consistency, patience, discipline, and commitment are the core elements of success for any trading method. You may use a valid technique, yet you won't succeed unless you correctly administer the rules. Mistakes can be made, and many poten-

---

1. See Bernstein, J., *The Investor's Quotient* (New York: Wiley, 1980), and *Beyond the Investor's Quotient* (New York: Wiley, 1986).

tial profits can be thrown away, regardless of whether long-term, short-term, or intermediate-term trading is your fare. The vital question is, "Can you make the commitment?" If you are not ready, willing, and able to implement a specific method or trading approach with discipline, consistency, and commitment, then I strongly recommend that you avoid cyclic trading or, for that matter, all trading systems, since they probably will not work for you regardless of the principles on which they are based.

For the short-term trader who is interested in making a commitment and in keeping it, a cyclic approach is certainly a good idea. Short-term cycles provide sufficient repetition and signals to give traders a good opportunity to test their ability to interpret signals and maintain self-discipline. The long-term investor requires even greater discipline and commitment, since his or her trading system requires thorough and consistent application of principles and techniques. Market entry signals must be acted on and not second-guessed. Objectives must be followed clearly and specifically without frequent deviation.

Long-term cycles may take many months to develop, and the urge to buy or sell too early preys on the mind of the trader. The undisciplined trader may give in to these feelings and clearly violate the basic principles of the system. Short-term traders guilty of such weakness realize their shortcomings much more quickly than long-term traders, which is one reason that I advise all investors to spend time and money educating themselves in short-term trading. Discipline will be acquired more quickly, and lessons will learned more thoroughly. Making a mistake several times a week rather than several times a year (that is, the short-term versus the long-term investor) certainly results in faster learning of important skills.

Therefore, in order to determine whether you can make the commitment to invest or trade using cyclic methods, do some soul-searching as well as hands-on practice and then make a commitment to either short-term or long-term trading.

Available Time

Another important variable in determining which system to use is time availability. You need to determine the amount of time you can invest before you make any commitments to the market. Don't consider trad-

ing for the very short term unless you are willing to make this a
full-time occupation. If you can't stay with a short-term trading approach by doing the technical work, then don't make the commitment
because you are sure to fail. Even a long-term approach is doomed to
failure if you cannot invest the time, regularly and without exception,
to keep your analyses current.

If you can't evaluate yourself based on the areas discussed in this
chapter, you may wish to take more time to think about significant
issues unique to your life. If your health is poor, for example, the intense
pressure of short-term trading is not advisable. Other considerations
may be professional, family, or educational commitments. Each has a
direct bearing on your individual situation and should be considered
when making your final decision.